7 SECRETS
OF RAISING
GIRLS EVERY PARENT MUST KNOW

**FROM BIRTH
TO 18 ONWARDS**

Judy Reith
founder of *Darling Daughters*

7 SECRETS OF RAISING GIRLS EVERY PARENT MUST KNOW

Vie Books is an imprint of Summersdale Publishers Ltd

Summersdale Publishers Ltd
46 West Street
Chichester
West Sussex
PO19 1RP
UK

www.summersdale.com

Printed and bound in the Czech Republic

ISBN: 978-1-84953-671-4

Substantial discounts on bulk quantities of Summersdale books are available to corporations, professional associations and other organisations. For details contact Nicky Douglas by telephone: +44 (0) 1243 756902, fax: +44 (0) 1243 786300 or email: nicky@summersdale.com.

For my darling daughters:
Phoebe, Tilly and Rosie

CONTENTS

FOREWORD

CEO and Founder of Mumsnet and Gransnet

Just over 15 years ago, I went from having no daughters to having two in the space of a few short hours. It's fair to say that the learning curve was a steep one: the early days passed in a blur of feeding, fretting and tearing my hair out at two in the morning when one or both of them wouldn't sleep. What I didn't anticipate a decade and a half ago, however, was how little that curve would flatten out. I assumed – oh, how naively – that once we were past those first intensive months, things would slowly become simpler. In fact, the opposite turned out to be true. We're now deep into the teenage years, and where initially, my daughters were defined by their age group – babies, toddlers, pre-schoolers – these days, things are different. They're no longer children; they're girls.

And raising girls brings with it a host of challenges from trying to explain why it's harder to be professional footballer if you're a girl up to the point when you're forced to the unpalatable realisation that when it comes to keeping them safe, both online and off, the issues are wider-ranging and more acute. Body image, technology, self-esteem and the pressure to succeed: the fact is that, even in 2015, it's different for girls.

All of which is why Judy Reith's book on raising daughters couldn't have come at a better time. Like Mumsnet, the website I founded for parents back in 2000, when my own daughters were just a year old, *7 Secrets of Raising Girls Every Parent Must Know* is fired by the belief that when it comes to children, there are no definitive answers – but that there are certain tips and tricks that could make all our lives easier, and that parents should share these wherever and whenever possible. Within its pages, she's unflinchingly honest about her personal doubts and difficulties when raising her three girls; she's quick to make clear that all of the advice she offers is given without judgment and that when it comes to children, the most useful thing any of us can do is leave our feelings of guilt at the door.

WELCOME

I have written *7 Secrets of Raising Girls Every Parent Must Know* to bring YOU the best seven secrets gathered from 24 years of parenting three daughters and from running courses, individual coaching sessions and giving talks to hundreds of parents who have wanted to transform their parenting. I hope that sharing this combination of personal and professional experience will bring a lifetime of benefits to you and your daughter.

You may have decided to read this book for a variety of reasons. Perhaps because you've reached a point where you're struggling to deal with your relationship with your daughter or the media have alerted you to the potential pitfalls of raising a daughter. Maybe you are anxious about what lies in the years ahead after noticing what is happening in families around you with older daughters.

Whatever the case, it's true to say that bringing up a daughter today can be considered a trickier task than that experienced by previous generations. In today's developed world, parents are under more pressure than ever to be A* parents producing perfect high-achieving A* daughters, who can shine in the modern world at work and at home.

Technology means we are all a click away from a global audience 24/7. This throws up issues that we've never had to face before, and all of this is coupled with huge pressures on our time. In addition to these guilt-inducing pressures, it's easy to get bogged down by the daily anxieties and irritations of raising a daughter. Many parents tell me they end their day, glass of wine in hand, feeling they have got it all wrong, yet they can't work out how to change tomorrow even if they did have the energy to do so.

If we throw these elements into the pot with the extra ingredient of how our daughters are facing issues different to those we might have known, we have a potent brew of concerns and conundrums for parents and daughters.

The daughters interviewed for this book feel the pressure, too. They question if they are pretty, thin enough or the best at gymnastics. Our girls are exhausted from what it takes to live up to the expectations placed upon them by the media, school, friends and parents. They also put pressure on themselves. Without the backbone of a decent set of values to live by, those values found in action at home, the pressures win. Unhappiness and low self-esteem take over causing girls to resort to seeking comfort from harmful people and harmful substances, which could leave lifelong scars. Parents find this frightening, so *7 Secrets of Raising Girls Every Parent Must Know* is here to help you find your way through these fears. Keep in mind with more equal and global opportunities on offer than in previous generations, it has also never been a better time to raise a daughter, with the more equal, global opportunities on offer to her.

" *Thank you Mum and Dad for a nice life; for looking after me and helping me always.* "

Lucy, aged seven

As a child, I couldn't wait to grow up and be a mum. The reality of parenthood was a shock. I remember being at home with two daughters under five and feeling unable to cope with their demands and arguments and my own sense of failure as a parent. I was often grumpy and prone to shouting and smacking, which was not at all the kind of parent I wanted to be. The thought of raising my daughters into adulthood was more of a burden than a joy. Something had to change. It's a long story, but talking to a mother who was getting help by attending a parenting course saved my sanity. I learnt new skills and an understanding of what parenting could be like without the shouting, smacking and sense of failure. It was like being forgiven and being offered the chance and the tools to start all over again. That huge relief to have some positive options that worked helped me to get rid of guilt and also spurred me on to train to teach parenting courses myself. Fifteen years later, I still find nothing more rewarding than helping parents gain confidence and ditch the guilt. I have learnt so much from the parents I have had the privilege to work with and from parenting my own daughters - it's time to share it.

It starts with asking you to pause for a moment, perhaps as you gaze at your daughter sleeping peacefully. Imagine what your daughter might be like in the future if she has the values and the tools to overcome all the potential pitfalls. Picture her in ten, twenty or thirty years from now and what do you see? A confident woman, able to navigate what life throws at her? Someone who is a pleasure, not a pain to live with? A woman who is fulfilled at work? Perhaps she has a family of her own - what kind of mother is she? Does she come to see her parents out of duty or out of love? *7 Secrets of Raising Girls Every Parent Must Know* asks you to start with the end in mind. It then becomes clearer what your priorities need to be, and that will drive your actions.

None of us knows how much time we have in which to help our daughters become fulfilled, grown women. If today were my last day, I hope I have left my daughters with a strong, clear set of values and skills with which to navigate the modern world without me. I want to leave my girls with values that reflect what's important in our family and its history. That is what will help your daughter best, and is what you will learn from reading *7 Secrets of Raising Girls Every Parent Must Know*.

One of the key things to note is that there is no perfect way to raise a daughter. You are the expert on your daughter, not me or any other parenting professional, medical professional, friend or family member. You will know best how to use the advice and stories I share in this book; what you can see working or at least what is worth a try.

> *Only parents really know what is the best possible solution for this specific little unit at this point in our family's lives. Being uncertain is part of that.*

Debbie, mum of two teenage daughters and a son

> *Trust your instincts – you know your girl better than anyone.*

Sarah, mum of two daughters aged 17 and 19

What's in the book, then?

7 Secrets of Raising Girls Every Parent Must Know is here to celebrate the opportunity to raise a daughter. I am passing on many ideas to you, framed into seven secrets, which have inspired me through my work with parents, over twenty years of being a mother and a lifetime of being a daughter. My own parenting experience is included, but to respect my daughters' privacy, I am sharing principles rather than too much detail of specific incidences. I will also share with you what all kinds of parents have found useful in developing their legacy to their daughters *and* what boosts their confidence to deal with the daily stuff.

My goal for writing this book is that it will be a fresh, fast and useful read as parents have so little spare time. Start where you like, but you'll probably get the most out of this book if you read it in order. The seven secrets' structure will help you to keep in mind what I believe to be the essentials to raise a daughter well. Put the secrets on the fridge door, tattoo them on your forehead, whatever it takes for you to recall them easily.

Write it down – make it happen

I've noticed that parenting habits are much more likely to change for the better when parents keep some notes, perhaps in a lovely journal, on the notes pages at the back of this book (pages 311-319) or digitally. Record what strikes a chord with you, what you could see helping you and your daughter. You might want to make some notes now about why you want to read this book. Commit to making changes, instead of just thinking that you might. Talk about it with your partner (if you have one). Talk about it with your daughter. I have found that leaving parenting books around and sharing online parenting links kicks off some interesting family discussions and sometimes a few arguments!

" *Listen and listen, don't try to find answers on their behalf. Ultimately they are their own person and what we may find helpful they may just find really irritating.* "

Ali, mum of a grown-up daughter and son

My Seven Secrets

Secret 1
CHANGE
Understand and prepare for how your daughter grows up

Secret 2
VALUES
Model your values – your legacy to your daughter

Secret 3
V-SIGNS
Know what is essential to keep your daughter safe and happy

Secret 4
DADS
Use your power wisely

Secret 5
MUMS
Ditch the guilt - be the role model you want her to have

Secret 6
VILLAGE
Build your village Create a community to help you and your daughter

Secret 7
PATIENCE
There is no rush

The secrets are out! They have been distilled from many years raising my daughters, researching and working with parents who have asked me, 'What's the secret to raising confident daughters?'

They are for you to share and I hope you will spread them generously. Read on to find out why they're so important and how they can benefit you and your daughter.

Words of wisdom

Alongside the secrets, you will find plenty of quotes and stories from parents. Some contributors' names you may recognise, but most have had their names changed.

At the end of each chapter, you will find a thought from someone who taught me a huge amount: my mother. She drove me mad at times, but her quiet wisdom, humour and patience nourished not only her own family, but also hundreds of other parents and children who loved her.

I know so many parents who really miss the support that local and able grandparents and other family members can offer. I hope sharing my mum's parenting ideas, wit and wisdom with you provides some comfort and inspiration.

Introducing Marmar

Marmar was my mother. She was given the name 'Marmar' by my first daughter who, when she was about a year old, attempted to say 'grandma', but what came out was 'Marmar'.

Her husband, family, friends, neighbours, colleagues and strangers called her Marmar for the rest of her life. She was a mother of three daughters – I am the middle-born one – and a grandmother to ten grandchildren by the time she died. Her parenting ideas were child-centred and she found much of the anxieties and the speed of modern parenting a great sadness. She would say to me, 'There's no rush. Can't you put your feet up?'

When raising my own daughters, she was always nearby, and not just because for years she lived 20 minutes away. In my mind, I still hear her reminding me to slow down, to live in the present and not to worry too much about the future. She was an expert at 'mindfulness' long before it became a best-selling concept. She lived by a set of timeless parenting values of kindness, wisdom, selflessness and patience.

I had eight years to adapt to the truth that I would eventually lose her due to her Alzheimer's diagnosis. The value of her legacy to me, and my daughters never really crossed my mind until her death.

I wrote this while visiting Marmar shortly before she died:

> **❝** *I am waiting for my mother to die. I sit beside her care home bed where she lies curled up like a child, just shrivelled skin and bones, eyes half open. Her heart is still beating; her lungs heave air in and out, and the rest of her organs are just about functioning. She cannot walk, speak or move. Goodness knows what is going on in her mind. She's been in the grip of Alzheimer's for eight years and along with my two sisters, I have been a most reluctant witness to her decline. They say hearing is the last sense to go, so I talk to her and tell her tales about my three daughters and what the weather is like on this November Monday. I sing 'You are my Sunshine' and an old hymn or two. I clutch a tear-soaked tissue, and wonder if any of this is going in, or is of any comfort, then I am reminded of someone*

advising me that when visiting Alzheimer's sufferers, 'In the moment you are there, it is a good thing.' So as I wait for her to set sail away from her daughters and towards her Maker, I have decided I must write about the many other moments when being her daughter has been a good thing. Fifty-three years of her influence and care. How she has been a light to guide me as a mother to my own three daughters, and enabled them to shine too. Beyond my family, she was a fountain of parenting wisdom, kindness, patience and mischief to dozens of other parents and kids. It's time to share what Marmar had to say on the subject of raising darling daughters, and I hope, as you read her words, maybe for you, it will be a good thing. **"**

Marmar breathed her last the next day. Just before, I whispered in her ear that I was writing this book, and that she would be in it.

" *If you've got nothing nice to say, say nothing.* **"**

Marmar

Housekeeping notes

Language used

We are raising daughters in all kinds of combinations of adults and children living together in a unit called a 'family'. Sometimes I will talk about partners, but I appreciate many are raising daughters alone. I do not intend to use language that might exclude anyone or cause offence.

I have spent many years trying to support and cheer on parents at a pace they can work with. At this point, I might need to be a bit bossy to save you time. I don't intend to sound like a headmistress.

Age and stage

I want this to be a useful book about raising daughters at whatever stage you're at, but the first secret is dedicated to having an understanding of what your daughter is experiencing as she grows up and how you can be prepared for that. It's important to note that my days of parenting my own three daughters are far from over. As I write, one has left home, one is at university and one is a teenager with several years left under our roof. I see parenting as 'a life's work in progress' with no solid definition of when the job is done. The 'Boomerang Generation' of adult children returning to live at home due to high housing costs, job shortages or relationship breakdowns is something I have not experienced so far, but I know many parents are in this position. Like any stage, it can benefit from pausing periodically to have an honest look at what's going on in the family. After that, a rethink and a conversation about what is needed and wanted by everyone in order to get along as best they can.

Resources

Given that there are so many types of families, some may need specialist help with developmental or behavioural issues. In the Directory (pages 253-265), I have listed websites, reading material and helplines which I believe are good resources, but in this fast-moving world it's essential you check them yourself. If you have any recommendations, or ideas that have helped you, please visit www.darlingdaughters.org and leave them on the Directory page.

Books and films
Watching films and TV programmes and reading books that contain great role models for girls can help inspire good values in your daughter. There are some suggestions for you in the Book and Movie Club (pages 265-270). It would be great if you could add to this via the Darling Daughters website: www.darlingdaughters.org.

66 *My parents always have time to listen to me. They never make me feel stupid for having an opinion or feeling a certain way. They're kind, generous, patient, and help me pursue my interests.* 99

Jess, aged 19

Task

Before the secrets are explained, take a few minutes to turn to page 279 of Parents' Notes and record your thoughts on *why* you have this book in your hands and *what* you want to learn from it.

SECRET 1: CHANGE

UNDERSTAND AND PREPARE FOR HOW YOUR DAUGHTER GROWS UP

" Time passes faster than you think. Don't get caught up in the little stuff, just enjoy your daughters as much as you can. They will all get to where they need to be in their own time. "

Lara, mum of two daughters aged seven and eight

There are five parts to this first secret –

Part 1 - Baby darlings, 0-2 years
Part 2 - Little darlings, 3-5 years
Part 3 - Little madams, 6-11 years
Part 4 - Young ladies, 12-16 years
Part 5 - Wonderful women, from 17 years

Each part is a straightforward guide to:

- What your daughter is experiencing at each stage.
- What your daughter needs from a mum and a dad.

I was in the loo, staring at the blue line on the pregnancy test that confirmed I was pregnant. I remember wondering how on earth a few cells multiplying inside me would somehow mature into a human being. My school biology lessons felt very distant and unclear, so like many parents to be, I bought a book with lots of pictures explaining the stages of pregnancy for mother and baby, and my husband and I went on a course of antenatal classes keen to learn how to tackle labour and birth.

Once she was born there wasn't much time to think about the theory of how she might develop from a baby to a toddler, a child, a teenager and finally into a grown woman. Child development and parenting books piled up beside my bed, but overwhelming tiredness often meant a magazine got a quick flick through instead. It wasn't until my girls were school age and my parenting studies began that learning about Mother Nature's part in their developmental stages became an essential part of my parenting toolkit.

Why?

Having some knowledge of what is happening to your daughter mentally, physically and emotionally will help you to better understand and deal with some of her behaviour that you might find difficult, bewildering or exhausting however old she is. That's why the first of my seven secrets is about change and about understanding and preparing for how your darling daughter grows up.

Child development is a vast topic that many experts, books and websites can expand for you; some of those that I have found to be the most useful are listed in the Directory at the back of the book.

This chapter presents my general guide, not a biology lesson, nor a nature *v* nurture debate. If you're short of time just zoom to the stage you're currently at with your daughter, but please bear in mind the following factors that will also influence her behaviour and her development at any time.

Your daughter is unique. There is no one else among the seven billion people on the planet who is exactly like her, even if she is an identical twin.

Her birth order position in the family. There are characteristics associated with birth order positions: only child, firstborn, middle born, last-born. For example, only children mature faster, firstborns tend to be more serious, middle-born children more adventurous and last-borns can have high levels of self-esteem. There are advantages and disadvantages in each position, and these are detailed for you in the birth order characteristics guide on pages 270–273.

Being the only girl in the family can influence how she sees herself and how the family treats her. A daughter who has only brothers as siblings may be more of a tomboy or may be particularly girlie, either of which she could have been naturally drawn to or had reinforced by parents, family and friends.

Having special or additional needs can have multiple behavioural impacts. As parents, we aim to treat our children in exactly the same way, but actually we don't. As each child is born, some things have changed.

We have changed. As we grow older, perhaps because we have more resources available to us or may have a different partner, our values and priorities can change. For example, who has lots of photos of their firstborns and hardly any of their younger children?

We are more confident. We're likely to be more relaxed and confident with second or subsequent children. Sleepless nights and the responsibility of being a parent have lost their shock value.

Who is she? We respond to the personality we see in our daughter. We respond to her gender and position in the family.

Parts of her personality that we may find challenging can remind us of a part of ourselves we have struggled with which can make us fearful and provoke strong reactions. For example, if you have battled with weight issues and see your daughter tucking into piles of chips, you may overreact. We make connections back to our birth order position and gender in our birth family, and look at how those affected our childhood.

Life events. We may have experienced a significant illness or bereavement in the family that can affect our mood and energy levels. It can also shift our values. We may feel time is running out, causing us to prioritise things differently.

> *Her older sister no longer wants to play with her like she used to and she really misses this. We seem to need to fill the gap emotionally and entertainment-wise in a new way.*

Hayley, mum of two girls aged 12 and 14

It's not fair!

A word about siblings

Some parents I meet use up huge amounts of time and energy trying to be fair to their children. How many chocolate buttons each child has, having the same toys, how much pocket money, what to spend on birthday presents and on it goes. If we keep trying to be fair, and we frequently talk about the importance of being fair, we're more likely to find our children shouting 'It's not fair!' back. I'm not suggesting it's a waste of time trying to treat your children as equally as you can, but aiming to be completely fair can be impossible when each child is unique.

However, I appreciate that when daughters (and sons) wail 'It's not fair!' it's annoying. If this is happening in your house, try:

- **Reflecting back thoughts and feelings.** 'You seem to think it's not fair I went shopping with your sister?'
- **Fantasy.** 'I expect you wish I had taken you shopping?'
- **Who needs what?** 'When you have finished your exams, what would you like to do?'
- **Letting them know that wailing doesn't win.** Children learn amazingly quickly what works to make their parents give in. If wailing and moaning means you pacify them by giving in and providing the treat or making promises you can't keep, they will use wailing next time they want something or they will say 'It's not fair!'

  Instead, try and remove yourself if you're likely to cave in. Leave the room or, if you can't, aim to rise above the wailing or moaning as if you couldn't hear it. Ask them what *they* are doing: 'I know you think it is unfair that your sister has a party this afternoon. What would you like to do while she is out?'

  Children also have to accept that the world is unfair. They are bound to come across family members, friends, teachers and employers who treat them unfairly. Let them know you understand how hard it is to feel you have been unfairly treated.

Children are unique – being fair is impossible!

Over time, you and they, and your circumstances can change. One thing that is always possible is to notice and celebrate what is different in each child. You could say something like: 'There is no one else in the world with your lovely blue eyes.'

I teach a six-week course on sibling rivalry, but here are my five favourite ways that will sort out most squabbles.

Step 1: Low-level bickering? Ignore the bickering. Instead tell your children you expect them to go and sort it out or to play separately. Remove yourself if you can, and tell them to come and find you when they have come up with a plan to solve the dispute.

Step 2: Moderate war? Help them to decide on a plan to get along nicely, or split them up for a while if they need to cool off first.

Step 3: Blood on the carpet? Split them up immediately, tend to the wounded and wait for everyone to calm down before you decide with them how best to proceed. Say that you will listen to both sides of the story, without interruptions from anyone. It may mean you're not sure who started what or who is being truthful. The important thing is to remind them of house rules (see Secret 2, page 70) such as 'being kind', and that hitting or hurting is definitely not 'being kind'. Broken house rules need to have consequences too, but they are only effective if you and your partner are consistent in applying them. You need to decide what behaviour in your family could result in a verbal warning, followed by sanctions if essential.

You might say something similar to: 'I have asked you both to stop arguing and agree what you're watching on TV. I am disappointed that you couldn't do this and Millie is in tears and Lucy is angry. I am turning the TV off and there will be no more TV today. I want you to apologise for hurting each other. Tomorrow, I want you to show me how you're going to choose what you watch without arguments and fights.'

Step 4: Reflect back feelings. 'I can see you're really cross that your sister took your hairbrush, but you must not hit her with it.'

Step 5: Insist on apologies.

BABY DARLINGS, 0–2 YEARS

'Who loves me? Am I safe?'

What's happening for your daughter?

In her **first year**, she will transform from multiplying cells to the early stages of toddling and trying out words. Physically, she will develop from a helpless tiny baby, carried with her head supported, and then pass the milestones of sitting up, crawling and first tentative steps. Her body and brain will grow faster in her first year than for the rest of her life, spurred on by lots of eating, sleeping, crying, wriggling and increasing mobility. In a few months she will progress from breast or bottle milk to three mushy meals a day. She will wee and poo her way through more than a thousand nappies.

She is subconsciously looking out for whom she can trust and feel safe with. Crying is her way of alerting you that something is upsetting her; it is the cry for attention because she has no words yet to let you know she is unhappy or uncomfortable.

In her **second year**, her increased mobility from crawling to walking will make her physically adventurous and you will need eyes and ears everywhere! Her daytime nap will be a welcome break for her and you.

She will be delightfully curious; happy to try eating worms or stick her fingers into plug sockets if you're not watching her! Nappies will gradually give way to potty training, with girls tending to get the hang of this earlier than boys. Other children will only be interesting in very short bursts.

She might resent you stopping her in her tracks or taking something away from her. When she is overwhelmed by big feelings she has no words for, she may wriggle, kick, scream and yell 'No!'

Your job

Firstly, it will help you if you recognise that your life as you knew it is over! I remember attending antenatal classes, but in those days the emphasis was on pregnancy and birth, and there was one session on 'Becoming a parent'. I have often thought since then that we needed far more lessons on being a parent, and that one or two on birth and labour would have been fine.

Becoming a parent is like going to the moon and never returning home. It's as exciting and as terrifying as that.

Tips for parents

Aim low: Do whatever you can to make life for you as gentle and uncomplicated as possible in those early months. You being relaxed and calm will give her the best start.

Love her: Psychologist and attachment theory pioneer John Bowlby helped me realise that it's impossible to spoil a baby with too much warmth, love and affection from someone who loves her. You need time to bond with her and immerse her in cuddles, smiles and kisses. Sing lullabies to her – gentle singing calms you as well as her.

Expect lots of **mess and horrible smells**: She will cover you, her and every surface you can think of with sticky, slimy smelly substances from inside her body. She will squish her food and then rub it on her face and hair or your face and hair.

Routine reaps rewards: When you are beyond tiredness, having a simple routine you and she are used to will be less stressful. Equally, something that helped me hugely was to see the clock as the servant not the master. Meals, bath time and bedtimes all had their slots, but having a flexible approach to time kept anxiety at bay.

If you have a partner, try and find a way to connect with each other. **Date nights are essential** if you can do it. We used to put the baby in the buggy and just go for a walk if we couldn't find a babysitter.

Forget expensive 'educational' toys. **Everything is educational.**

> " *Go easy on yourself, don't try and do everything yourself and be perfect, good enough is OK.* "
>
> Olivia, mum of a nine-month-old daughter

Mums

Having a baby or a toddler is exhausting. Feeling so tired that I felt faint is the one thing I remember most as it affected everything. After a few weeks, I started working part-time from home, helped by my firstborn being a regular deep sleeper (she still is). I am very aware of the guilt, stress and anxiety suffered by many parents, especially mums, who have to return to work sooner than they would want. If this is you, then make the most of your non-working hours to prioritise enjoying your daughter. If you don't have to rush back to work, treasure your time with your baby daughter, as you will never have this time with her again. It can be a bit boring being surrounded by baby chaos and looking like you've spent the day on the allotment, but it won't last. Making some time for you without her is also time well spent. Accept any offers of help – meals, babysitting, hand-me-down clothes, toys or equipment. Get out every day if you can – even five minutes of fresh air and exercise will lift your spirits. Meeting up with other parents can be a lifesaver, but keep your distance from parents who seem to be perfect or critical of you. They could ultimately dent your confidence.

Dads

Your partner is having a baby, and you can feel redundant. She will need lots of love, patience and reassurance from you, and actually you need the same, but she might not be able to give you that for a while.

In those first two years, lots of dads say they feel like a spare part. Sometimes your partner can make it worse for you by being critical of your attempts to help. I am sorry; this must make you feel useless. You are so valuable to your baby daughter and as she grows up. The fourth secret is all about helping you make the most of your unique role in her life from day one onwards. She needs you to hold her, cuddle her, change her, feed her and take her out with you even if she is yelling 'MUUUUMMMMMM!' when you attempt to pick her up. There is a lot you can do to support your partner, too. What helped me the most was my husband just listening to my incoherent ramblings and uncertainties. He understood that was as valuable to me as offering domestic or childcare help – that and providing chocolate.

What would Marmar do?

Marmar's patience with babies and toddlers was mesmerising to observe. She would calm down a hysterical toddler with one of her made-up songs or a soothing lullaby. Sometimes sung, often whistled, and accompanied with a gentle back rub.

LITTLE DARLINGS, 3–5 YEARS

'Playtime!'

66 *When I was little, hours would go by playing at her kitchen sink taking apart old teabags, or pouring dishwater into assorted plastic cups and jugs.* 99

Marmar's granddaughter, Tilly

What's happening for your daughter?

She's on the move, and there is a whole world out there for her to discover. She will want to explore everything with her hands, feet, mouth, eyes and ears. Let her go probably a little further than you dare, as learning to take a few risks will be good for both of you. If you stop her, she may get nasty and shout, scream or lash out. She'll be experiencing different environments at nursery and in other homes, but she will want her own home to be a calm base to return to after her adventures.

Her imagination will be limitless, helping her brain to grow. She doesn't need to be surrounded by the latest toys for her development to thrive.

> ❝ *To invent, you need a good imagination and a pile of junk.* ❞
>
> Thomas Edison, best known for inventing the light bulb

Her curiosity will produce a never-ending stream of chatter, ideas, requests and questions. A girl's speech generally develops earlier than boys, and throughout her life she'll probably stay ahead of the boys with her range of vocabulary and the number of hours per day she spends talking.

Let her...

... get out there! Explore her environment and find out what it is like to be messy, dirty, hot or cold without anyone worrying about her appearance or telling her girls shouldn't play this way.

... wear herself out. Her body and her mind will flourish being adventurous and creative out of doors. Let her run, dance, cartwheel and skip, whether she's dressed as a fairy, a pirate or in dad's old jumper. Expect bruises and scabby knees from lots of tumbles. Marmar used to pick me up each time I fell on my knees and say warmly, 'Are you saying your prayers again, Judy?' Had she rushed up anxiously fussing over me and asking where it hurt, studies show I would have been more likely to cry and be upset for longer.

... play with anything! Junk, packaging, huge cardboard boxes or old clothes are just as much fun as expensive toys.

... watch TV and limit play on computers. Screens can be addictive even to a little darling. Limit the time she is allowed on electronic devices and explain your rules to grandparents, babysitters and older siblings who might look after her.

... meet and make friends. Open your door and let them in. Friends will help her to develop a wide network where she can grow her social skills.

> *" I love the way she wants to be twirled around by me endlessly, her love of music of all sorts. Exploring her body anywhere, anytime through balancing, headstands, roly-polies, jumping, skipping... "*

Natasha, mum of two young daughters

Starting pre-school and school

Choosing nurseries and schools can cause parents to move house, take out a bank loan and have sleepless nights, but it doesn't need to be so stressful. Choice of schools can be the problem as well as the answer. Girls are likely to be more ready to start pre-school than boys as they develop the social, emotional and mental skills needed earlier.

You need to do your homework and visit pre-schools with her, and not just on their open days. Talk her through in simple steps what her day will involve. Make sure she understands instructions such as: 'Before playtime', 'Put your shoes on' and 'Hang up your coat'. This may sound obvious, and you know your daughter best, but teachers report an alarming increase in children arriving at pre-school and school unable to follow basic instructions. Be prepared for her to be really tired out by the school routine, and possibly cranky when she comes home. Taking a snack along at pick up time made all the difference to my daughter's mood on the way home.

Tips for parents

Cheer her on! Encourage her, be interested in everything and respond to dramas without a fuss; be disinterested in toys promoting image, fashion dolls and princesses, etc. She may gravitate towards these, or be given them by friends and family, but if you show your enthusiasm for gender-neutral toys she will notice that. She might prefer pink, but in my experience it doesn't last.

66 *Don't be neurotic about pink.
Sometimes, it's just a colour.* 99

Tim, dad of two daughters aged two
and eight and a stepson

Fill a crate with junk. Collect things that she can make into anything she wants, and save a fortune on sophisticated toys. Likewise rummage in a charity shop or use your own old clothes to create a dressing-up box.

Expose her to the fascinating **world of nature**, placing creepy crawlies in her tiny hands before she thinks they're scary. Marmar taught me how to make a daisy chain – it was quite fiddly splitting the stem of a daisy before threading in the next daisy, but I loved showing my daughters how to do this too.

66 *Never help a child with a task at
which he feels he can succeed.* 99

Maria Montessori, pre-school educator and expert

Gradually introduce her to simple chores. Laying the table, helping with laundry, watering plants, picking up food wrappers from the floor of the car or tidying shoes are all chores that can be done by three-year-olds. (See Chores your daughter can do and when, pages 277–279.)

Be consistent. She needs to feel that the main rules are the same no matter who is looking after her. It's really hard sometimes to be consistent.

Looking after yourself and supporting each other will give you both more strength to face the harder side of parenting a young daughter.

Talk to her about the qualities of friendship. Tell her what you like about your friends, such as the way they listen to you, have fun with you or care about you when you're unhappy. Please avoid labelling her by saying 'She is shy' as labels reinforce behaviour. If she demonstrates unkindness, you can take her to one side and say that's not how we treat other people, and ask her how she would feel if someone treated her that way. (There is more about friends and friendship throughout the book.)

> " *I remember investing in beautiful pyjamas for her so that if it had been one of those hideous days, putting her in those soft pyjamas when she smelled lovely after her bath helped me end the day on a happier note!* "
>
> Julia, mum of a grown-up daughter and two sons

Mums

When I run a Darling Daughters live event, I ask parents to consider what they would say to those in the room with younger daughters if they could go back in time. Without exception, they say to those parents with three-to five-year-olds: 'Just enjoy it.' When I think back to my own darlings being at this stage, I notice that I automatically smile. Yes, it was tiring and demanding juggling small children, work, a home and other relationships, but that is not what dominates my memories. Looking back at photos of them then, sometimes in matching outfits, reminds me of their zest for life and fits of giggles, more than squabbles and tantrums. At the same time, it can be hard to enjoy it non-stop when little darlings want their mum's undivided attention.

> 66 *Allow them some choice, so they feel in control. Read/paint/play with them. They crave your undivided attention.* 99

Katy, mum of Polly aged three

Your daughter is beginning to notice she will grow up to be a woman, like you. That's why it's fun to try on your clothes and copy what you do and say. Our job of being a role model starts very early, but we're human beings with our own needs to meet too, not some kind of super mum. Katy is right. Enjoy your daughter's company, and be a little girl again by playing with her. Daughters thrive when they experience you relax, laugh, play and be carefree. She does this naturally, a delightful role model for us without knowing it.

Dads

In your daughter's eyes, you are enormous. You are maybe three times her height, and your voice is deep and loud. You might have a prickly face and be much more hairy all over than Mummy. You have a lot of power, even if it doesn't feel like it sometimes.

What matters most is that she can see past the physical side of you, and sense from your words and actions that you are a kind and hearted dad. You're also up for rough and tumble and tickling sessions. Explain to her that if she kicks you in the balls it really hurts! She could reject you and say, 'Go away, I want Mummy!' It's normal for her to do this – try not to take it personally, complain or tell her off for this. She is naturally testing boundaries. Have a go at engaging her by showing your curiosity in a game or a toy, or ask her what she had for breakfast – anything that takes your mind off feeling useless or resentful. Bedtime story reading could be your thing, as it has always been for Simon Mayo, author and radio presenter.

66 *Reading the bedtime story became my thing. My complete repertoire of voices (posh, Cockney, Cornish and camp) works for every kid's book ever written. And I loved it. I looked forward to story time probably more than the children.* 99

Simon Mayo, father of a grown-up daughter and son and a teenage son

LITTLE MADAMS, 6–11 YEARS

'Be my best friend?'

(By the way, calling your daughter a 'little madam' is a label - please avoid!)

I think it's important to recognise that a little girl of six will change greatly by the time she's 11. Therefore, some of this stage will be split into six to eight and nine to 11. Remember, age is only a guide; you know your daughter best, so do use any parts of this secret that you feel resonates best with you and your daughter.

In my junior school years, I spent a lot of time upside down doing handstands against the playground wall. This was between bouts of French skipping with friends or juggling tennis balls. At some point the handstands stopped when it dawned on me that being upside down meant my knickers were on show. I went from being a carefree girl keen to perfect a handstand to being uncomfortably aware of a new feeling called embarrassment. From there, embarrassment took over, leading to shyness and a lack of confidence in my body, especially as it was beginning to change. By the last year of primary school, hair was appearing in funny places and the hair on my head would look greasy even a day after washing it. One girl in our year got her first bra and her period, but I didn't really know what it all meant.

The changes a girl experiences in these junior school years bewilder and delight her and her parents. She enters this stage a young carefree girl, though by the time she leaves it she is on her way to becoming a woman. At school, and perhaps at home if she has older sisters, she will be aware of what changes are to come, but until she's around ten, there is a lot of fun to be had as a child. I loved this stage with my own daughters – a delightful blend of growing independence, curiosity and emerging personalities. My third daughter was born when her sisters were five and eight, and although challenging at times the upside was she provided a wonderful way to keep us all childlike for longer.

" *These are the Golden Years. I love the conversations I have with my girls. They laugh a lot. They still like doing things with the family. And I can still snuggle them. But it is so interesting and gratifying to watch them grow and develop and become more mature.* "

Laura, mum of two daughters aged seven and nine

What is happening to your daughter...

... between the ages of six and eight?

Friends: They will increasingly be her focus. She could fall out with them over the colour of a hair clip, but be best friends again in minutes. Invitations to play dates, parties and sleepovers will take on huge significance.

School: By now, school will be a solid base for her to learn and make friends. She might start to become aware of how she measures up to others' abilities and say something like, 'I can't draw' or 'I can't do maths.' (See Tips for parents on page 40 for more on this.)

Hobbies and interests: These are great years in which to try different activities such as music, art, dance, drama and sports. She is curious and she has free time after school. At the same time, keep some blank spaces in her diary in which to do nothing or to be spontaneous.

... between the ages of nine and 11?

Friends and social media: In his great book *Ten Conversations You Must Have With Your Son*, headmaster Dr Tim Hawkes writes about looking out of his window at break time and seeing the girls at this stage are sitting and chatting in small groups, while the boys charge around until the bell goes. Girls are sociable creatures who like to chat, but as devices such as mobiles or tablets are given to younger children, they will love socialising via selfies, texting, Instagram and Facebook, (even though Facebook is officially for children from 13 years onwards.) They will be using technology at school and at home, and are probably more computer literate than their parents. I took my first selfie aged 52.

Moving up to secondary school: Remember what that felt like? Where her friends are going will matter to her probably more than what the school has to offer.

She will notice **different values** in other families. Who is allowed what, where and when, from chocolate cereal to ear piercings, bedtimes and swearing.

Her feelings: These will be surfacing as her hormones begin to wake up, causing anything from moodiness to hysteria. She can be sensitive and reactionary. A cuddle on your lap can end in seconds because you innocently said the 'wrong' thing or your breath smells.

Puberty begins: She has to cope with breasts developing, pubic hair, spots and then periods. Her moods will start to swing from happy and carefree to grumpy or anxious, maybe without any clear reasons why.

Tips for parents

> Our job is not so much to make our daughter happy, but to help her deal with unhappiness.

Welcome her friends and model the qualities of a decent non-judgemental friend when you're with your own friends. Help her to manage conflict and unkindness from friends. (I will show you how in Secret 4, pages 164–184.)

Take her feelings seriously by listening to her and responding accordingly, 'That sounds sad, it's hard not to be invited to Milly's party.' If she says she can't do something, such as a maths sum or a sport, encourage her by using a word like 'yet' which offers potential. You could say something like, 'You're trying hard, and you haven't found the way to do those sums yet.'

Voice your own feelings, so she learns it's OK to talk about feelings. Use the word 'I'.

Comment positively where possible. For example, if there are shoes all over the hallway, in the first instance, go for a positive comment such as 'It's much easier to find your shoes when you put them away tidily in the hall.' However, if it's an ongoing problem, you could add how it makes you feel too. 'I feel fed up about the shoes everywhere in the hallway. It looks much better when you tidy them away and they are easier to find.' A negative response would be: 'You're so untidy, you never put your shoes away!'

Talk about what your family stands for, and how other families have different values. Don't assume she'll just pick this up; sometimes you have to spell it out: 'In our family we do our best to make friends feel welcome by sharing our home with them, and being interested in how they are.'

Go with HER passions and interests, and enjoy them with her - it's not a competition. Help her to experience activities such as sports or drama clubs, which include boys, especially if she is at a girl's school or doesn't have brothers. Some girls want to do everything on offer. As well as what she has time for, consider what your time and budget can support that keeps things varied: perhaps one sport, one arts and one social club.

Make the most of any travel opportunities before academic work takes over. If you can't afford to travel far, open up the world to her with travel books, programmes and websites. Try out different foods from all over the world. Use Google Translate to say 'I love bananas' in ten different languages with her.

... from age eight onwards?

Puberty? Do your homework! I will help you with this in Secret 4 (see pages 164-184), but the principle you need is to be open to talking about it. Check she has sanitary products in her school bag as well as at home. Support her growing body and mind with healthy food and making sure she gets good sleep. Think about the old slogan for Mars bars - 'Work, Rest and Play' - she needs all three (but not too many Mars bars!).

Boost her independence and her self-esteem by *asking for her opinion before giving your own.*

Give her more responsibility, but you'll need to teach her first. You probably did it this way with brushing teeth, and it's a good model for teaching most things. I remember we showed our daughters how to use a sharp knife to cut up carrots by making a bridge shape with their hand over the carrot to safely control both the knife and the carrot! (See Chores your daughter can do and when, on pages 277-279.)

2. YOU show her how to do it

1. YOU do it for her

3. SHE does it with you beside her

4. SHE does it

Be a bit selfish sometimes. Keep looking after yourself. Keep some regular time to catch up with your partner.

" Don't project your own views/interests on to your daughter assuming that she will share them – your daughter is not always a chip off your block. "

Sarah, mum of two daughters aged eight and ten, and a four-year-old son

Mums

Marmar was at home full time until I was ten. She found a part-time job in a local office once my younger sister started school. It was comforting to have her around at home during those years, and when my own daughters were this age, I was fortunate to have an interesting part-time job working from home. Combining working and parenting are big pulls on a mother's time, energy and heartstrings, and it can be difficult to find the right mix of the two. It's hard being aware your daughter is watching you, but she will learn valuable life skills from how you deal with the complexities of working, being a mum and everything else you do. In these years, she is likely to openly adore you, write you beautiful notes and happily hug and kiss you. Every Mother's Day you will be told you are the best mummy in the world. Take delight in her before she enters her teens and will naturally pull away from you.

> *" Enjoy her. Enjoy the ability to choose her clothes and do her hair. Allow her to play football and take ballet lessons and remember to cuddle her as much as you can because a time will come when that allowance will no longer be given. "*

Rosie, mum of two girls aged eight and ten and a three-year-old son

Dads

You are important in your daughter's life at any time, but especially in these middle years when you may feel she doesn't seem to need your support or you wonder how to relate to her. Stick around –

please don't give up. I have met plenty of dads who find these years are the best with their daughter. She's out of nappies and outgrown toddler strops, but she hasn't hit the teen years yet. She is capable of having a go at just about anything. Dads with older daughters look back on these years with great affection as a time when their daughter didn't find them embarrassing or boring.

> 66 *My dad is really imaginative and when my mum is busy after supper, Dad, me and my brother have hilarious conversations.* 99
>
> Amber, aged ten

You have a great opportunity to put the time in now to build up some good memories for both of you to draw on in the future. My husband and our daughters have many fond recollections of when he would drive them to school. They would practise spellings, sing along to the radio or simply sit silently sometimes holding hands in crawling traffic. Your best bet is to show some curiosity as genuinely as you can in what her interests are, even if they're not your thing. She needs to feel you are her number one fan. You can do that by giving her uninterrupted time, by listening to her and asking her questions before jumping in with your own answers. (I will explore this more in Secret 4, page 164-184.) Compliment her on how she uses her mind rather than what she looks like. Saying to her 'I love to watch you swim' will light her up far more than telling her she's the best swimmer. Make plans with her to do stuff together, just the two of you, before that's the last thing she would want to do.

> *" I love her very deeply. I have big dreams for her, but they come second to her dreams for herself. "*

Andy, dad of an 11-year-old daughter
and a two-year-old son

What would Marmar do?

 Marmar was a great mender, recycler and knitter. She taught her daughters and her granddaughters how to knit with her little rhyme:

> *" Make a kiss*
> *Bring the wool right round like this*
> *Slide it, slide it up through the hole, and off! "*

Her mending pile was a colourful collection of socks, gloves, my dad's pants, anything with a missing button and various unidentifiable items. She would watch TV and mend something at the same time. I remember her thimble being too big for my fingers, but I loved playing with it and her sewing basket – both of which I still use.

> *" Marmar mended anything made of fabric, including my brother's underpants, which she took back to the UK once to add to her mending stash. "*

Marmar's granddaughter Marie, who lives in New Zealand

YOUNG LADIES, 12–16 YEARS

'You're so embarrassing!'

> " *I wasn't expecting my 12-year-old to be so 'teenage' this early (from 11 years). I struggle with her wanting to be so adult – in her dress and manner, etc.* "

Val, mum of two daughters aged ten and 12

At the younger end of this stage, a girl is still a child, but not quite a teenager. The media have invented new terms for these children: 'tweenies' or 'tweenagers'. It is a twilight time of relentless change and uncertainty that can carry on all the way through to adulthood. Remind yourself what you felt like at secondary school as you made your way up from being a first year to being part of the management, if they made you a prefect.

My big passion as a teenager was pop music, which my dad dismissed universally as 'That awful boom-chicka-boom' whether it was The Who or David Essex. Increasingly, my parents didn't understand me, and I found them annoying and embarrassing. However, they did support me to join a local drama club. I loved spotting them in the audience when they came to shows and pantomimes. Having that drama club helped divert me away from chasing after boys and illicit smoking at the local park. I decided I wanted to be an actress, a career choice that didn't go down well at home or at school. These years are when a girl is discovering what she loves, what her values are and what she can learn if she takes a risk. For me, it also included my first kiss and my first cigarette.

When my girls reached these years, I think the hardest thing was being unprepared for how little time we would have together as they, and we, were busy. I also found it tough trying to accept that they needed to pull away from me and discover their own set of values, which would mean some arguments and anxieties. We had our share of struggles, and although my professional knowledge of adolescence was a great help, there were times when they felt misunderstood. Fear of the unknown caused trouble for me. How much to insist on homework standards, healthy eating or technology usage could cause me to overreact instead of using my pause button to make a more measured decision. At the same time, having teenage daughters was fun and invigorating. Their opinions, music, friends and energy roared round the house like a jet engine. The house was littered with clothes, and hair and make-up products jostled for space alongside guitars, ballet shoes and bikes. I remember their mad laughter and also their tears when it all got too much. At those times, I tried to remember that one of the best ways you can comfort an upset daughter is to sit and listen, even if every part of you is resisting that.

66 *Listen to your daughters and treat them like real people. Be respectful that they probably won't want to be treated like a toddler when they are a teenager.* 99

Jade, aged 14

What is happening for your daughter?

Her brain is undergoing a major reorganisation as it cuts back on what it doesn't want, and strengthens what it needs. It won't be fully formed until she's about 25. Until then, brain development can cause her to be impulsive, rebellious, to lack empathy and to make decisions and solve problems emotionally rather than rationally. Therefore some unusual behaviour is normal.

I love doing... ? What does she love to do apart from being with her friends? Steve Biddulph in his excellent book *Raising Girls* refers to this as 'Spark'. From dance to debating, baking to ball games, or camping to clarinets, it's the best time to do something that may require persistence. She needs to experience that effort pays off. It can be tough, but if you want her to learn and enjoy activities such as sport, art or music, hunt around for the most inspirational teachers you can find to make those lessons, and the practice, as positive as possible. One of my daughters learnt the trumpet for a few years with a woman who surrounded her with encouragement, praise and a lot of laughs. We all enjoyed those trumpet lessons.

Money: As her independence grows, she might want more money to fund her hobbies and interests. Pocket money can give way to a regular allowance, which you need to negotiate with her, and together you should write down what she is expected to pay for out of the allowance. She could earn some money babysitting, car cleaning or dog walking. It's a good idea to have a list of jobs that you're prepared to pay for. Marmar taught us to divide our money into thirds, which she called the three Ss:

S for spending
S for sharing
S for saving

" *Something else I'll always be grateful to my parents for is having my own bank account when I was around age 14. Rather than giving pocket money or paying for my classes and lessons (tennis, piano, etc) they would put an allowance into my account on the first of each month and I would have to make my money last the month paying for cosmetics, haircuts, hobbies, extra-curricular classes, etc which taught me how to save and spend wisely.* "

Tara, aged 25

The **pressure of school and exams** will build and anxiety can take over. She may lose interest in making an effort, or fail to see the point of working. If this happens, it may be a temporary blip, but make sure you ask her school for their side of the story, and for their support.

Private, keep out or 'go away' are clues that she is doing her growing up. Needing to pull away from her parents is important and normal development.

" *My dad often asks me what I'm thinking, and almost always, I would rather not share. I think that your thoughts are kind of like your diary, and someone else cannot demand for a diary entry at any time :)* "

Lucy, aged 14

She will be **trying to cope** with everything that puberty throws at her. Periods, pubic hair, breasts, spots, grease and smells from hormone surges that also send her mood out of control.

Her mind can be in turmoil as she wrestles with the **'Who am I?'** question. Even a seemingly happy upbeat girl can have thoughts more like Eeyore. If we could listen in, it might sound something like this, with each 'ping' meaning she's checking her social media:

> *I don't care, I hate my parents, ping, I'm depressed, I feel great, I want to sleep for a week, my dog's the best, I'm ugly, I'm fat, I'm useless, ping, I hate school, I'm rubbish at maths, I've got no friends, Tom's hot, ping, maybe I fancy Haley????, what is God? I don't know, I'm broke, ping, shit, I'm late!*

Peers: What her friends think of her really matters and staying connected to them on social media is essential to her, even if you think she's just messing about on her phone.

She is sensitive. She will be much more self-conscious about her appearance, what your house is like, and what you look like and what you say.

Crush time and falling in love with someone you're never going to meet. As I write, it's the boy band One Direction (1D) that is giving girls heartache and sleepless nights. By the time you're reading this, I suspect 1D will have been replaced. That first crush can be all consuming. You can persuade yourself that there really could be a future for you (in my case, David Essex), if only he could meet you. So, aged 14, I wrote to David Essex offering to babysit for his children. He still hasn't replied.

Drinks, drugs, sex, piercings and parties will all come her way, even if it's just via a PSHE (Personal, Social and Health Education) lesson at school. She will be alongside girls who are interested in experimenting with illegal substances and behaviours that are potentially harmful. Just wait for Secret 3.

Speaking of which, **self-harm.** Whether it's an eating disorder, cutting or anything else that is done to cause deliberate harm, your daughter could be self-harming or could know someone who is. I don't want to frighten you, but it's essential to be aware that some girls are self-harming, especially in their teens, as an outlet for their painful feelings.

> " Coming home after school to a cold, empty house as a teenager wasn't nice. "
>
> Sarah, grown up and recalling her teen years

Eighty per cent of the parents I coach have teenagers. It is a difficult and challenging time for parents when they feel at a loss to know how to cope with their teenage daughter (or son). Plus, teenagers get such a bad press with frequent studies underlining just how bad teenagers are, or how neglectful their parents are. Extended family can criticise your parenting and say unhelpful things like, 'Why do you let her talk to you like that?'

There is so much criticism and scaremongering about teenage girls, it's time to champion their good side. Teenage girls can be hilarious balls of fun and energy and they can help us to lighten up and not take parenting so seriously.

You have a great opportunity to boost her confidence, which in her teen years can wobble at any moment. As well as telling her yourself, let your daughter overhear you saying to family, friends, teachers and strangers what you admire about her.

" Try and give as much confidence as you can to them. Tell them often that they are doing well, and that they are special in their own way. "

Jenny, two daughters aged ten and 14

Tips for parents

Live out your values. Don't leave it to the fridge magnets for her to figure out what your family stands for. I'll show you how to do this in the second secret.

Believe in her, even when sometimes she will struggle to believe in herself.

Support HER passion as enthusiastically as you can. You won't have to be a taxi service forever or the audience member, but these moments are also opportunities to spend time with her, listen to her and encourage her.

Create a loving base to come home to. My daughter told me leaving a friendly note and a lamp, the radio and the heating on was really appreciated when she came home to an empty house. If you're in, stop what you're doing and go and say hello to her as if she was a friend coming to visit. She might reject a kiss and hug, but don't stop offering them.

She might be grumpy. She's had to keep up appearances and deal with school life all day, so might not be the jolliest company at home. Someone once said to me that the people we love get the best and the worst of us.

Familiar routines such as meals, chores or family occasions are reassuring when she is uncertain about herself, who she is and her future, or is obsessed with her own thoughts, feelings and actions. She needs to know what the house rules are on chores, bedtimes and screen time. She also needs to pull her weight and not get out of her share of helping out because you think it's easier to do it yourself than face a fight.

Family meals and cooking together help you both to keep in touch and to talk and listen. These times are not lecturing opportunities. Roast dinners were greeted with enthusiasm in our house and kept us all at the table.

Your communication with her will move towards negotiations, but **you don't have to know all the answers**. Pausing and saying 'I want to think about that' means that you take her seriously and it gives you time to work out your response.

Trust: She is likely to want you to trust her with managing her time, homework, diary, money, food – just about everything. Trust is a two-way process. She needs to be able to trust you and know she can rely on you.

Arguments: It is time for her to pull away and find her independence, and rebellion is a perfectly normal way to do this. Keep an eye on the ratio of how many positive things compared to negative things you say to her in a day. Ideally it should be ten positives for every one negative. A girl can take something you say, such as an innocent question as criticism or an attack, even if that was the last thing on your mind.

> Parent: *'What time are you coming home?'*
> Daughter: *'You're ruining my life!'*

Keep up the fun. It's so sad hearing from parents who say they no longer have fun with their daughter or that she doesn't want to do anything with them, and so they give up offering. It's understandable; it's hard to keep giving when your offers are greeted with eye rolling or worse. But our job is to hold onto the hope that one day, she will change her mind. We won't get to see that if we've given up. In the meantime, do what you can to not let her bad mood or behaviour dominate the family. Having that much power will be destructive for her too. Enjoy yourself and let her see you laugh and be positive in spite of the enormity of trying to raise a family, work and manage a million other things.

Help needed. Sometimes there is little payback in these years and it's very hard to live with a daughter who is making family life a nightmare of raised voices and slammed doors. Spread the load by finding other good role models, whose values are similar to yours, to influence her. This is what I call 'your village' and we will build it together in Secret 6.

> 66 *My sister is younger than me, and because she's not their mother, she just enjoyed my daughters being teenagers, which helped all of us.* 99
>
> Claire, three daughters aged 12, 15 and 19

Mums

Many mums have told me that these early teenage years can be pretty dire. They feel their daughter has changed overnight into a monster that rejects her mum. On top of rejection, some daughters take up criticising their mum about how she looks, what her opinions are, her cooking, her interests. It feels almost like grief, and it really hurts. She takes the piss out of you in front of other people, leaving you lost for words and staggered that she can treat you like this. If you're living with this abuse, it's much harder to find the energy to be a good role model yourself. If it is of any comfort, this is a phase your daughter is going through, and she will grow out of it. Your job is to recognise what things you can ignore and what things you feel you need to challenge. It's time to gather the family and brush up house rules, particularly those relating to how you treat and speak to each other, as well as whose turn it is to take the rubbish out.

She is watching you like a hawk. Something she can learn from you is how you make decisions around self-discipline at a time when her decision-making will be very impulsive. For example: 'I'd love some new winter boots, but my old ones are fine. They just need re-heeling and a clean.' You may think like this, but it's great for your daughter to hear out loud how you make decisions.

Dads

I was on a train recently and sharing the carriage with drunken men returning from a football match. Fortunately, their team had won so they were opening the beers and keen to have a chat with me, the only woman in the carriage, even though I was nearly old enough to be their mother. I felt a bit anxious, but we got round to talking about family and kids. They were dreading getting home as their wives 'never listen and just give them a mouthful'. They also decided I needed to hear what a pain their teenage daughters were. I was curious to know why they thought their daughters were a pain. Here is what one of those dads said:

> ❝ They're so moody, I just don't get it. With my son, if he's in a mood, he'll just hit something or kick a ball, and it's over with. With my daughter, it goes on for days. My sister was just the same. ❞

Sound familiar? Without wanting to peddle the stereotype about dads not understanding their teenage daughters, this is a frequent tale I hear from dads and it can be the excuse they use to give up on their daughters. That's the last thing their daughters need. It is fundamental that you rise above the moodiness or rejection and persist in showing her you still value her. If you don't do that, then she will look elsewhere for respect and approval from men, perhaps the kind of men that get drunk on trains or worse.

Instead, focus on these teenage years as ones where she needs to experience you as her number one fan. Some dads just do this, but if you're finding it hard, please don't give up. Use this book, your mates, your partner, your sister, colleagues or anyone who can help you know what to do and can give you support. Finding help is a sign of strength, not weakness, and evidence that you are a loving dad.

WONDERFUL WOMEN, FROM 17 YEARS

'I must fly'

This is the last section on how your daughter grows up. It includes completing education and leaving home, but with an increasing number of children returning to live at home as adults, it's hard to know when they will have finally left. I couldn't wait to leave school or home. I remember in those last couple of years at home the embarrassment about my parents had calmed down, but I didn't feel that close to either of them. I wouldn't have dreamt of confiding in them – that's what my friends were for.

Two of my daughters have been through this stage. Those sixth-form years saw them both have mixed experiences of school, university applications and relationship highs and lows. Exam pressure seemed relentless. Family holidays often involved lugging books and laptops along so they could keep up with schoolwork. Listening carefully, more than advising or suggesting, still remained the best way of helping them to sort out their dilemmas or challenging behaviours. That and an endless supply of tea, eggs on toast and a Sunday roast. Once they went off to university, keeping in touch by Skype was great, but I know they also loved receiving hand written cards and unexpected 'care packages' of favourite treats along with medical supplies and multi vitamins.

What is happening for your daughter?

She is on her way to **increasing independence**, but she's not there yet, even though UK law says she is old enough at 16 to have sex and therefore to become a parent. She can marry with permission from her parents, but she isn't old enough to drink champagne at her wedding. She can't vote, or go to a film with an 18 certificate, but she can raise a child. At 17, she can drive a car or a motorbike. These are just some of the ways in which your daughter is seen by the current UK legal system to be able to take control of her own life. But you know her best. She may be legally able to do these things, but is she ready?

She might embark on her first steady **relationship.** She might have found someone whom she deeply loves, and this could last a lifetime. I know several couples, still together after 40 years, who started dating in their teens. A break up of an intense relationship could be devastating and the pain of it can take weeks to ease.

> 66 *A lady's imagination is very rapid. It jumps from admiration to love and from love to matrimony in a moment.* 99
>
> Jane Austen, *Pride and Prejudice*

Is she having **sex?** She could be under pressure to do so and not be ready for it. Is she **gay or transgender?** If she is, it is likely that she will struggle to come to terms with this, let alone how to come out to her family and friends.

Exams take over. Currently in the UK, there are public exams for three years – GCSE, AS level and then A level. There will be pressure on her to achieve her grades all the way through. She may have applied to a sixth form college or to a university and received offers requiring certain grades. This makes the workload relentless, there is always the next piece of homework or coursework to complete. Results' day can be a celebration or a nightmare if she doesn't get the grades she needs.

She will still be grappling with her 'Who Am I?' questions of her earlier teens, but a new school for sixth form can be a fresh start, a chance to meet different people and to re-think who she is and what's important to her.

Career options will be up for debate as she looks at courses and career paths. It's difficult for girls who feel they should know what they want to do by now. One career for life is not how they are taught. I remember going to a parents' evening when my eldest started secondary school back in 2002, where the head teacher explained that the curriculum was designed to meet the expectation that our children would, on average, change careers five times during their working lives.

Home is a place to sleep, be fed, have clean washing appear on your bed, and where she can ask for lifts and cash. Her bedroom is more like a bedsit, unless she has parents who insist she still eats together with the family. If there are not enough cash hand-outs, she might have to get a **job** as she realises how much it costs to buy clothes, make-up, go to festivals and concerts, or buy alcohol or illegal substances. At 16 (18 upwards if alcohol is sold), she is old enough to work in a shop or a cafe. She might have set her sights on a **gap year** which would require serious money, but all that planning, working, saving and travelling will give her great life skills.

Your job

In my daughter's first week at university, a person on her landing was trying to make supper from one of those pots of instant noodles. They put the whole lot, including the pot, in the kettle. When I heard that story, my first thought was what kind of parent let his or her child leave home without basic cooking skills? My second, more generous thought was that this person had been raised on home-cooked food and had never come across instant noodles before!

Your daughter is likely to be really busy; you won't see her much. She will spend a lot of time in her room with the door shut when she is at home. Carry on being a **loving base** where friends are still welcome. Teenage parties need a clear set of rules, and I would say with parents being under the same roof being one of them.

House rules still apply, but keeping up the relationship using empathy, cups of tea and clear communication is key.

> *I understand you're tired after netball, and you have a mountain of homework; it's still your turn to clear up after supper.*

Tips for parents

Hand on more responsibility. Your job is to help her to be a pleasure not a pain to live with. Teach her how to cook, use the washing machine, clean her room, plan her travel and manage her money.

> *In my first term at uni, I put my dirty laundry in the machine with detergent and switched it on and left the room. I went back later to collect it, amazed to find it dry already, but there were blue streaks of detergent on my clothes. Turns out I had just baked my clothes in a tumble dryer.*

Lucy, aged 19

Don't rely on cooking skills being taught in enough detail at school. Instead, aim to teach your daughter to cook at least ten different meals that can be adapted. School holidays may be an easier time to do this, but if you taught her a recipe a week, she could quickly build up a list of recipes that she can make and adapt. A roast chicken is far more economical to buy than chicken pieces. Leftovers can be used to make risotto, curry, a pie or pasta dish and the stock can be used for soup.

Show her the household bills. Show her how fast the electricity meter whizzes round when her hair straighteners are plugged in or when she tumble-dries a top that she wants to wear in half an hour.

Talk to her about what kind of woman she wants to be. Who does she admire and why? TV or radio programmes, plays, books or media articles can be a good place to spark these questions. Now is the time to call in favours from the family, godparents and friends who can provide work experience, another perspective on adulthood or a listening ear.

She might be in a relationship, or not, but if she is sexually active I would encourage you to talk to her about what she is using for contraception and to protect herself from sexually transmitted diseases. Recognise that it's normal for parents to have mixed feelings about their daughter having sex. Owning up to your embarrassment is better than avoiding the conversation, and it may 'break the ice' between you. Talk with your partner about house rules for partners staying overnight. You might need to talk to her partner's parents about what you are prepared to allow.

> " A couple with older children are the first
> in my tribe of friends to wade into the murky
> waters of puberty, and they have done it without
> a single wince. They maintain their gentleness

throughout all the awkward sex conversations,
as well as the huge emotional outbursts. 🙶

Jen, mum of a five-year-old daughter

Affirm her qualities and talents when she is talking about courses and career options. Expect her to research her post-school options – it's her who is going, not you! (Sorry, I have seen too many parents taking over and doing all the research.) For example, if she wants to study geography, it is much more helpful if she compares how courses differ and how the university location affects what they can offer before she talks it through with you.

Be a coach, which means show an interest and ask questions rather than providing answers. For example, ask her how she is getting on with her UCAS form, instead of filling it in for her or writing her personal statement. Outside of school, any **volunteering** opportunities she can lock into are fantastic in helping her gain work experience and giving her time to those in need. She is still likely to be self-conscious and will have a tendency to be self-obsessed. An hour a week volunteering in a care home can help her put her own concerns into perspective compared to the needs of elderly people. In addition, this kind of volunteering will enrich her CV or college application.

Enjoy her when she is around instead of pouncing on her with a lecture, a list of complaints or thinking you haven't got time to chat. She'll be gone before you know it.

Mums

In these final years of your darling being under your roof, the good news is that she is less likely to have a go at you just because you exist. As she matures, you could be treated to some kindnesses you thought had long gone as she starts to ask how you are, or asks for your opinion. If you are not experiencing this yet, try to hold on, get your own needs met and never give up hope that in time your relationship with her will improve. What matters most is that she can think of you as her mum, not her friend – she chooses her friends. She needs you to be there to talk to. She wants you to listen quietly and not judge or criticise her. She may not want your advice either. If you can see she's really struggling to come up with a plan, you could say something like: 'I guess if I was in your shoes I might write down everything I need to revise for and see which parts are the hardest.'

66 *Always listen if you want to be listened to yourself. And always respect for the same reason.* 99

Janice, mum of two daughters aged 16 and 18

Unfortunately, she might want to talk late at night when it's the last thing you have the energy for. As I write, I'm thinking back to this time with my own daughters and there are tears splashing on my keyboard. My tears remind me that I wish I had known then just how fast that time would go. If I could turn back the clock, I would have said 'no' more often to my inclination to fill the diary. I would have kept more blank spaces, freeing up time to be around my girls while they were still at home so I could listen to their worries, hopes and emerging opinions or catch their laughter while we made supper during a tea towel flicking fight.

Dads

I have met many dads who find these last few years of having their daughter at home quite tough. Some dads feel at a loss to know what their job is. You could ask your partner what her dad did, or didn't do, when she was this age that was helpful to her. Seeing your 'little girl' almost grown up, considering her future and in a loving relationship can make you proud and delighted she's turning out well. However, it's normal to feel rejected, sad, redundant and even jealous when she is more interested in her boyfriend and has her whole life in front of her. **Acknowledging how you feel** is the first step to taking action. If you can, share your feelings with your partner, friends or family, but don't burden your daughter with negative feelings about how she is growing up and leaving home. Tell her you are proud of her, and tell her why. Tell her what you admire about her, and how much you're looking forward to hearing about her plans for her future. You may feel anxious she is not reaching her potential or that she is not ready to leave, but is that really true, or is it that you're not ready to let her go?

There is a strong chance that your relationship with your daughter will become more enjoyable as she matures. You both realise time together under the same roof is running out.

Before she does go, there is still plenty for you to do. She may be untidy, moody and ignore you, but your job is to act your age, not hers, and rise above most of her challenging behaviour. Remember the 10:1 rule – for every one thing you say that's negative, she needs ten positives. She needs to leave home with a clear set of memories about her dad being a decent man who loves and respects her that are demonstrated by giving his time and interest in her, not just his money.

Sometimes I feel like I'm just a walking wallet.

Andy, dad of a 17-year-old daughter

Spend time with her

If she's considering further education and needs a lift to college open days, it's a great time to share a journey, and to chat to her about what kind of future she is hoping for, and what she needs to get there. Take her to work with you if you can, or talk to her about what you find valuable in the work you do, or would like to do, that isn't just about earning money.

See if you can find something to do together, even if it's just a coffee once a week. The message you are giving her is that you're **interested in her** and want to spend time with her. You may feel you have lost any power or control, but you are powerful just because you are her dad. In Secret 4, I will show you how to use that power wisely.

She needs to know you are willing to trust her. She needs your encouragement, not your criticism. She needs to believe you are confident in her abilities to run her own life.

" Have the confidence in your convictions. Have the confidence in their ability and innate common sense. "

John, father of one daughter now aged 28

That's what you have been working towards since she took her first breath.

So that is the first secret:

Change:
Understand and prepare for how your
darling daughter grows up.

A parent's story about change

    ❝ *I have two daughters, Jess aged nine and Lucy aged seven. Until last year, they were good friends, mostly, with a few upsets over toys or attention from me or their dad. Recently, Jess started being really mean to Lucy and calling her 'a silly baby' and not letting her in her room. I found it really hard seeing this nasty side of her coming out together with the sadness in Lucy, as she adores her big sister. My partner lost his job last month so the atmosphere at home has been pretty tense, which didn't help my lack of patience in dealing with my daughter's behaviour. I shouted at her, took away her TV and tablet time, and begged her to stop being mean to Lucy, but nothing seemed to work. It was only when I talked to my sister who has older kids that I realised that Jess is growing older, she needs her own space and that she is old enough to be affected by her dad losing his job. I think I'm so used to just lumping them together as 'the girls' that I hadn't noticed it was time to start letting Jess grow up. My sister suggested I made a start by separating their bedtimes and that half term would be a good time to make the change. So we told them both that as Jess was now nine, and needing a bit less sleep, she would go to bed 20 minutes later like her cousins do. Lucy was a bit cross. We said we were sorry this upset her, but at the same time, lots of families do this and she would* *still have lovely stories and cuddles when she went to bed. We have done this for two weeks and it has been brilliant! Jess loves that extra time to be up with us and behaves like an angel. The other night, I had a chat with her about her feelings about Lucy, her dad's situation and what could we do to help her. She admitted she felt bad about being mean to Lucy, but she did feel Lucy was more annoying than fun, and she was worried about dad. It was such a relief for both of us to be honest, and she has been much more tolerant of Lucy ever since. Lucy moaned for the first three nights, but we held our nerve and she is fine now. I'm so glad I made the effort to make some changes; it's been good for all of us.* 99

Polly, mum of two daughters aged seven and nine

I'm including Polly's story because it illustrates honest, yet constructive parenting, and the value of taking action as follows:

- Polly realised the impact on Jess of growing up and of her dad losing his job.
- She decided to talk to her sister about it to get some insight from someone with older daughters.
- She felt, and expressed empathy towards Lucy, but at the same time stuck to her plan.
- She made time to have a chat to Jess without Lucy. It sounds like she listened well, as Jess felt able to open up and express how she felt.

During your lifetime of being a parent, your role will develop and move towards an adult-to-adult relationship with your daughter, which may include her becoming a mother. I hope there is a bright and positive future ahead for you and your daughter built from years of mutual learning to respect, trust and love each other. Whatever age your daughter is now, I want to invite you to consider the questions below and record your thoughts about them in your notebook or on the notes pages at the back of this book.

* What do you enjoy about having a daughter at her current stage of development?

* What are the biggest challenges?

* What's the one thing you would pass on to a parent with a child in the previous age group to the one you're in now?

Parents get so stuck in the dramas of daily life and find it hard to see past them to the bigger picture of what they really want their daughter's upbringing to be like. A question I have asked parents interviewed for this book is: What do you hope your daughter will remember about you when she has grown up?

> 66 *My miraculous longevity. Failing that, someone who loved her at every second and with every fibre of his being. (True).* 99

Tim, dad of two daughters and a stepson

> 66 *I'd like her to look back on a happy childhood, and to feel confident about herself and her abilities. I'd like her to know how much she is loved and adored.* 99

Marnie, mum to one baby daughter

How would you answer the question?

If you would like to share your answers with others, please visit the forum on www.darlingdaughters.org

What would Marmar do?

 No matter what stage my daughters were at, if I talked to Marmar about parenting concerns she would usually say: 'Oh, don't worry, it will be alright.'

Mostly, she was right.

REMINDER

Take out of this secret what you feel is right for you and your daughter.

SECRET 2: VALUES

LIVE BY YOUR LEGACY TO YOUR DAUGHTER

In this section, you will discover the secrets of:
- Defining your legacy to your daughter.
- How values drive behaviour.
- What to do when you and your partner disagree on how to parent your daughter.
- How to model your values and practise what you preach.

> *I hope she will have fond memories of her childhood and will aspire to pass on those magic things to her own children. That is the legacy down the generations.*

Liz, mum of one grown-up daughter
and two grown-up sons

What do you want your parenting story to be?

When you're old and grey, you will have time on your hands to think back over the years of raising your daughter. It's been said that nobody gets to their deathbed and wishes they had spent more time at the office. Most of us wish we had spent more time with our family instead of frittering it away on less important things.

Bronnie Ware, a nurse in Australia counselled many people in the last few days of their lives. At this time they often talked about their regrets and from this, she wrote *The Top Five Regrets of the Dying* (Hay House, 2012). The top two regrets that I noticed were:

1. I wish I'd had the courage to live a life true to myself, not the life others expected of me.
2. I wish I hadn't worked so hard.

Many of us lead a life that is not how we really want it to be, or one that is 'true to myself'. Part of my work is Life Coaching, and I ask my clients to write down their life goals. With parents, I also ask, 'What are your parenting goals?' and 'What kind of parent do you really want to be?' Do you think your job is, as the pioneer of the polio vaccine Dr Jonas Salk said, 'To give their children roots and wings. Roots to know where home is, wings to fly away and exercise what's been taught them.'

I think of parenting as a story that I'm writing without knowing what the ending will be. What will the story of your parenting be? Where does your story start and what happens as it unfolds? What kind of ending do you hope for?

Parents say they want to be loving and kind to their children, but they also talk about teaching them morals and giving them good values to live by. They hope their children will grow up to be decent, content and responsible citizens who, in turn, will be loving partners and parents. Is that what you want? Is it possible, or just another thing to feel guilty about?

If we do want that 'story' for our daughters, then it starts with the kind of life we're living now. We can start our parenting story again today, and decide what we want to put in it.

Imagine: The Perfect Parent of a Daughter.

What is that parent like? When I ask this at Darling Daughters live events, here are some of the words that the audience call out:

loving **rich** flexible
available **honest** reliable
role model helpful **cool**
fun **thoughtful** wise
energetic listens
patient **trustworthy**
fair kind

This parent doesn't exist, and attempting to be like this 'perfect parent' makes us tired and guilty. Sometimes, you have the energy to be fun, sometimes you're just too tired or simply can't be bothered. Sometimes you can be patient, and at other times you explode over something seemingly trivial, like waiting for your daughter to find her shoes. However, I bet that some of the time, not every day but perhaps more often than you give yourself credit for, the words above do describe you.

Do you want to write a better parenting story? It starts with you investigating what your parenting values are and how they drive your behaviour.

Where do our values come from?

Values spring from a variety of sources. Some we inherited from the way our parents raised us, and some are learned from other influential players in our childhood, such as teachers or religious groups. Throughout our lives our values can change and adapt according to who or what we love, where we live and in what society we find ourselves.

I believe our values shift when we become parents. We focus sharply on what matters most to us, and ask deeper questions about family, morality and spirituality. No longer just seeking to look after ourselves, and a partner, we are faced with responsibility and love for this newborn child, which can drive us to want to make the world a better place. Becoming a parent for me sparked an interest in education and climate change, a desire to be a good neighbour and a friend, and a more appreciative daughter to my ageing parents.

Working out your values

The first step to passing on your values to your daughter is to make sure you know what your values are. This will help you to make better decisions and write a better story in how you live your life as a parent. You may have a rough idea, but I have found writing these values down helps clarify them. Here's an exercise to help you do that.

Have a go at filling in the blanks with ten different individual qualities that you would want to describe your parenting. You might want to look at the jumble of words above to give you some ideas.

For example, 'As a parent, I want to be *reliable*.' Write your words on this page or on the notes pages (see page 280).

Ask your partner to do this separately, and then you could compare answers.

As a parent, I want to be...

YOUR NAME HERE:..

1...
2...
3...
4...
5...
6...
7...
8...
9...
10..

Our values are influenced by how we were raised, as Lesley's story indicates.

A parent's story about values

66 *I have two children, my daughter who's three and a baby son. I suffer from huge amounts of guilt that I am not a good enough mum, especially to my daughter because I shout at her, I criticise her and I just find her so difficult.*

I'm sure it's got worse because I'm so exhausted. I think she's jealous of the baby, but she's fine with him thank goodness. I end up in tears most afternoons after yet more battles with her, and sometimes my husband has to take a day off work to help me. The heart of the problem I realise comes from the way my mum treated me. She was cold and critical, and even now, my extended family will look at my daughter and say, 'She just needs a good slap,' which I hate, but I admit I have slapped her sometimes. I really really want to make sure my daughter doesn't look back on her childhood with sadness and unhappy memories. So I have decided that I'm not going to let history repeat itself. I am working out with my husband how we want to bring up our kids, instead of feeling so down about my parents and their opinions. I feel lighter and freer now, and it's been good to have a decent conversation with my husband about what really matters to us, what we want to keep from our childhood upbringing to pass on to our kids and what we're letting go of. My relationship with my daughter is improving – I just need to get to bed earlier! 99

Lesley, mum of a daughter aged three and a baby son

I have included Lesley's story because she has been honest with herself, and her husband, about her frustrations, anxieties and her exhaustion, but that hasn't stopped her making some changes as follows:

• Realising the impact on her energy and confidence of poor sleep and the demands of a young child and a new baby.

- Choosing to refocus on creating a happy childhood for her daughter and not letting history repeat itself.
- Involving her husband by asking for his practical help, but also to create together a shared vision of how they want to raise their children.

Your goals need to match your values

'Shoulding'

'Shoulding' is a verb I have made up. Parents do a lot of shoulding with internal thoughts and feelings and these become actions or goals, which don't always match our values. 'I should be home by now, I should be careful, I should be calmer, I shouldn't shout, I should drink less. I should know how to deal with this.'

'Shoulding' is usually a paralysing, guilt-inducing voice in your head that needs to be told where to go. With values, it's important to work out what **your** parenting values are, not what you think they 'should' be. For example, you may think you 'should' be honest, but actually you're not that concerned about bending the truth, white lies or just lies! Look at the list again and make sure they are YOUR values, not ones you think you should have or the ones that your partner, your parents, the 'perfect parent' or anyone else says you 'should' have.

Dear me, when I'm old

If you're not a list kind of person, you could write a letter or a story, or draw a diagram or a picture to your 'future' self to help you sort out the kind of parenting legacy you want to leave behind for your daughter. If you have a son, you could think about what other values you might want to pass on to him, for example teaching him to be respectful of women.

" *Try to give them a sense of what you think is important in life. Talk to them and explain your reasons for things. Have fun with them.* "

Sarah, mum of three daughters and a son

Does your life reflect your values?

I know nothing about you, except you probably have a daughter. I have no idea what kind of person you are, your age, who you live with, what your home is like, what you do for work, how you might vote or if you are religious. Would I meet you at a football game or find you on a market stall? What kind of music do you listen to?

Perhaps you're out tonight at a school committee meeting. How about a quiet night in watching TV? Turns out, it's a children's charity telethon - are you making a donation?

Did I see you popping in to say hello to that old lady up the road? Are you visiting family on Sunday after a tidy up in the garden or after a run? Is that one of your paintings in the hallway? How was the play last night? Did you have a good time when your friends came over for a barbeque? Who won the argument about state schools versus private schools? You got paid this week - what will you spend your money on? Are you the only one who notices the place is a tip and that the loo roll has run out? What's for tea? Fancy a drink?

I have no idea how you would answer any of those questions, but if I did, it would paint a picture for me of what is important to you and how you prioritise your resources of time and money. It would also tell me something about what you believe matters. Your children are growing up watching you live out your life in the daily detail that I have described a glimpse of above. Girls are particularly sensitive. I wonder what your daughter would say if I asked her what is important to her mum and dad.

> *" My mum sometimes gets angry with me for things she does herself, which I find extremely unfair. "*

Laura, aged 11

The big question is, if you took a snapshot of your parenting today, would your values be alive and kicking, or just words?

Consider those values you wrote down and think about how much you're satisfied with how they show up in your parenting. You might want to score them out of ten. For example, if you wrote 'kind' as a value you want to be as parent, you could rate yourself from:

10/10: 'I am completely satisfied with how kind I am as a parent' down to

0/10: 'I am unkind; I can't think of any examples where I show kindness to my daughter.'

Score your values out of ten.

> *" I struggle with feelings of guilt and am not confident that I am parenting well. I do better when I focus on her and don't compare myself to other parents, or the way people say things should be done. "*

Rachel, mother of a two-year-old daughter

Any value that scores less than five probably needs some attention.

Consider what YOU want to do that's achievable that will boost your scores. Why? Because…

… values drive behaviour.

When a value we hold dear is disrespected or neglected, we get upset, angry and say or do things we regret, and then feel guilty.

If you want to be kind and you shout too much, then you feel upset and disappointed in yourself. Why do you end up shouting when you really want to be a kind parent? I know what that feels like. I have shouted at my daughters. It could be when other factors interfere like tiredness, hunger, hormones or illness, but as an adult I know these are fixable reasons for shouting. Most parents I work with also identify these factors, and it's important to do that, but it's much more energising to focus on the values you want to model as a parent.

Tips for parents

Here are ten ways to focus on our values when they're challenged. I know that these tips work for parents, but feel free to add your own and share them with the rest of us at www.darlingdaughters.org

Calm yourself

1. Pause - leave the room, go outside or close your eyes, breathe deeply.
2. Meet a physical need – check for hunger, thirst, tiredness or the need for exercise.
3. Ask yourself, 'Why do I feel so strongly about this?' and 'Is it me, is it something I have inherited or is it a "shoulding"?'
4. Write down how you feel or talk it over with someone you trust.
5. Forgive yourself. You're a human being not a saint.

Dealing with difficult stuff

6. Acknowledge that your daughter is her own person entitled to her own set of values, which may or may not be the same as yours.
7. At the same time, she is part of the family. Decide what you're prepared to let go of, and what you feel you really must hold on to. Talk about this with your partner.
8. Focus on what you love about her, instead of the things that make you cross or disapproving.

9. Depending on her age, talk with her about what has upset you and why you think it is of importance, using an 'I' not a 'you'.

10. Be more than willing to listen to her without interruption or judgement.

Using the word 'I' instead of 'you' is a clear assertive way to express your needs without shaming or accusing your daughter. 'I' is the smallest word with the greatest impact. 'I want you to be honest with me about how much homework you have' is clear and straightforward in comparison to: 'You never tell me how much homework you have.'

Tip

Remember to use

'I'

Your daughter's values

I have a powerful memory of being about 17 and getting into a heated argument with my dad about racism. I was tentatively challenging his view – quite a bold step for me in those days.

He made a sweeping generalisation about a country that was home to one of my friends. I looked him in the eye like a wild dog and said, 'I have no respect for you saying that.'

He flew into a rage, bellowing at me: 'What? You don't respect me? You have to respect me!'

I pushed past him and ran out of the house and didn't come back for hours.

A clear example of a father and daughter realising that their values were clashing head on, causing fury on both sides. Re-telling that still makes me feel uncomfortable. In an ideal world, he could have responded better if he had been able to acknowledge that I was growing my own set of values. He could have turned this into a conversation or a debate instead of a row.

How about your daughter?

Does her life reflect the kind of values you want to see? The Jesuits have a saying: 'Show me the child until he's seven, and I'll show you the man.' This would suggest that parents have the first seven years to be the major influence in how their child will turn out. Even at seven years old, you'll begin to see how your daughter is making her own set of values and questioning the ones she has been raised with. (She should do this; it's normal development.) If your daughter is older than seven, it's not too late. References to age in this book are a guide, not a certainty!

With any luck you may be fine with her moral compass. She's a decent girl with a good attitude to most things. But perhaps you're like most parents; some anxiety is creeping in. Are you worried about her friends? You've noticed she's started answering back, staying in her room a lot or constantly texting. She loves lasagne, but she only picked at it last night. She spends far too much time online; goodness knows what she sees in those YouTube clips. Surely her school marks would be better if she applied herself. At least she's still having piano lessons. What if she gets into trouble - how would we know, what would our parents think? She's avoiding us - we're a close family aren't we? And on it goes - an endless flow of typical anxious thoughts that a parent has about how their daughter is living her life.

When we see behaviour in our daughter that shows disrespect for a value we consider important, we can react strongly, which may come across as a disproportionate response.

You might shout something like: 'Stop teasing your brother, you're being really unkind to him.' But what if your partner is there and he or she doesn't even notice that your daughter is teasing her brother? You feel you're the only one in the family promoting kindness as a family value. Mums and dads disagreeing on family values creates arguments, resentment and can even cause couples to part. How wide is the gap between you and your partner on how to bring up your daughter?

Mind the gap

" *Talk about your fears, doubts and beliefs about how best to bring her up with your partner (or whoever you are closest too). Getting validation from someone else can be reassuring and ensures that your daughter doesn't receive mixed messages.* "

Nikki, mum of a daughter aged
two and a half and a son

Most of us have children without having conversations about how we want to bring them up. It's only when we're in the throes of parenting that we see the cracks appearing in our assumptions we made about each other as parents.

" *I thought we would agree more about how to bring up our daughters; this is not really what I signed up for.* "

James, dad of two daughters aged three and five

Whether it's manners, discipline, education, religion, finance or hobbies, or even what to spend on birthday presents, we can find ourselves feeling disbelief that someone we love and have had a child with is not the kind of parent we expected. The parenting story we're leaving to our daughter turns out not to be in the same book, let alone on the same page.

From daughters dressed in pink to how late they can stay out, parents can argue about how to bring up their daughter. This has always been the case, but in our fast-moving, stressful society, a recent national newspaper report cited that there are more than 20 different 'family' combinations of adults and children living together. With the confusion and exhaustion this creates, it is more important than ever to find, and respect, some core values and rules you can agree on among the key adults who are raising a daughter regardless of their age, relationship, sexual preference or ethnicity.

What is your starting point?

From the moment you know you're pregnant you will wonder if you're having a boy or a girl. I wanted a healthy baby, and I admit I hoped for a daughter first time round. When you and your partner start out on the long road of raising a girl, you will both bring your own experience of girls on that journey. Mums, of course, approach raising a girl with their own experience of being one. Dads will have their view on daughters coloured by any sisters, friends and family. Even if we're trying our best for sexual equality, it's easy to fall into the trap of stereotyping girls based on our starting points.

Try this: What goes through your mind if I ask you to complete these two statements?

'Girls should…'

'Girls are…'

Are generalised views of girls a source of disagreement between you and your partner?

Find your way to write your parenting story together

A difference of opinion or even some disagreement between you and your partner is normal and can be healthy. It gives your daughter a wider experience of what's important and drives behaviour. For example, one of you might think adventure is essential. I would never have prioritised saving up to take our children to South Africa to visit a street child project like my husband did. This trip where we met kids on the street with nothing like the advantages our children have, changed our lives. Our daughters tell us it was the best childhood experience we gave them.

Imagine what it would be like if you could reduce the disagreements? Imagine having a useful conversation with your partner in which you both wrote together a shared story of life lessons that you want to pass on to your daughter.

Single parenting

I know and work with many single parents, but I don't have first-hand experience apart from fleeting times when my husband has been away for more than a week, and it was a great relief when he came home again. Without exception, I take my hat off to those raising their children alone as best they can under stressful circumstances. I appreciate the ideal would be that after the relationship breaks down, you are able to communicate in a civilised manner and agree over how to raise your children. For some, this is unimaginable. Here are a few tips for single parents, and there are extra resources in the Directory (see page 258). If you have tips you want to share, please go to the parents forum at www.darlingdaughters.org

The widowed parents I have met are the most courageous I have come across. If you're in this situation, I hope you are being comforted with the right support around you. Grief cannot be ignored or rushed, and every family will have a unique story. There are some great organisations listed in the Directory that are gifted and experienced at helping you and your child.

Tips for single parents

- Have high hopes and low expectations that you will find ways to agree with your ex-partner on some basic values that you both want to pass on to your daughter, even if it's too difficult to contemplate in the early stages of separation.
- Get help and support from those who understand what you're going through and can do so without judgement.
- Explain to your child that these are the rules in your house, even if it's completely different in your ex's house.
- Seek mediation if you need to. Even if your ex-partner refuses, seek help yourself to manage your feelings.
- Avoid criticising your ex in front of the children – take your pain, sadness, frustration and anger elsewhere.
- Listen to your children if they are hurt or upset. In their adolescent years, they may refuse to keep contact with the absent parent. Encourage them to send an email or text or to write a card if they don't want to see the absent parent.
- If you're the rejected parent, please continue to offer contact, including texts, cards and emails, even if they bounce or are returned unopened.
- Build your village of supporters and role models for your daughter. I will show you how in Secret 6.

When the British actor Bob Hoskins died, his daughter Rosa paid tribute to her dad thanking him for 11 life lessons he had made sure he gave her.

The life lessons were: laugh; be yourself; be flamboyant; don't worry about other people's opinions; whatever you do, always give it a good go; be generous and kind because you can't take it with you; appreciate beauty; take pictures and make memories; don't take yourself too seriously; never, ever, ever, ever give up; and love with all your heart.

Ask yourselves this big question, separately, and then compare answers. Your answers should not include money, housing or anything else that comes with a barcode!

If this was your last day as her parent, what life lessons or advice would you want to make sure you had passed on to your daughter?

Make notes separately and then together. Which ones are the most important life lessons that you both agree to pass on to your daughter?

If you find that a hard question to answer together, then you could consider it from your daughter's point of view. In interviewing lots of daughters for this book, I asked them what they wanted to thank their parents for. Here are some of their answers. What do you hope your daughter would say?

> " *I want to thank my mum and dad for showing me that life can be about so much more than the pursuit of wealth. And that the wealth of friendship and love is worth more than anything else in the world.* "

Connie, aged 20

> " *For being a stable happy family that very rarely argues. For making us have dinner all together. For letting me be different. For making me feel lucky to have you.* "

Alice, aged 17

> *Watching me do my show 'Gymnastics' (on a mattress at home) :) and my splits.*

Ellie, aged seven

> *Bringing my sister and me up on her own. I think Mum's amazing for doing just that.*

Beth, aged 21

> *I love that I find my parents very approachable about many different things – I can always talk to them if there's something on my mind. They are also very relaxed about letting me do things – so long as they know where I am, when I'll be back and that I'm safe and happy, they'll let me do most things!!*

Bella, aged 16

Make those values alive, not just words on a fridge magnet

Only kind words spoken here!

I believe you have done something very important in thinking about your values as parents and writing your parenting story to your daughter, separately and together. You have worked out what values you can't bear to live without, and those about which you are more flexible. Like Bob Hoskins did, you have created the life lessons you want to leave your daughter with both now and when you are gone. Together, these form a simple set of family rules as defined by you and they're much more relevant on your fridge than those magnets.

The next step is to make sure the legacy of those core parenting values are brought into the heart of your day, not lost in the swill of no time, stress and guilt.

In our family, remembering the needs of other people is a value we try to action. As our daughters have grown up and gone, those of us left at home miss them, especially at mealtimes.

Light a candle

A simple idea that we have found helps us to remember others and to be grateful for what we have is to light a candle at meals. We started this when our eldest daughter went away on her gap year travels, and we wanted to find a way to acknowledge that we were all missing her. Just before we eat, each person at the table names someone who is in need or a family member who can't be with us. It helps all of us forget ourselves and consider others just for a moment.

Ten tips to bring your values to life

1. Write your values down, draw them or create something, like our mealtime candle, that symbolises your values.
2. Say them out loud – often.
3. Be transparent. Ask your family what they think of your values list – this is guaranteed to produce a lively conversation!
4. Consider other families whose values you admire and see them as inspiration, and remember to ask your daughter (and any other siblings) who they admire and why.
5. Decide how you want to communicate your values (practise what you preach). Your daughter will notice far more about what you do than what you say.

6. Atmosphere – what kind of atmosphere do you want in your home? Warmth? Acceptance? A loving base? Choose to create that.

7. Activities – what kind of things do you want to do that represent your values? Keep a note of them and commit to doing them. Not everyone can go to South Africa, but being adventurous can happen every day if you want it to.

8. Watch films, read books and talk about news items that represent the values that you're keen to promote. (See Book and Movie Club on pages 265-270.)

9. Look after yourself. The truth is, you can't be kind or respectful when you're hungry, tired or stressed.

10. Stop the moaning, and start writing a better parenting story instead.

Parenting goes on for decades, so please don't feel it's a crisis if you have days as I do when it all goes horribly wrong or you simply can't be bothered. I heard the American singer Bruce Springsteen say that the amazing thing about children is that they come with an infinite pot of grace to forgive us. Thank God.

" I remind myself that I am trying to do my best and that we all make mistakes – it is important to be able to say sorry and to let your daughters see that you are a flawed, vulnerable person too, but that together you can work things out. "

Jo, mother of three daughters

What would Marmar do?

 Although I was born in Australia, I spent most of my childhood in a suburb of North London where my New Zealand-born parents were unusual compared to the neighbours. Their lives could be described in the 1970s as mildly eccentric, driving a battered old Morris Minor when they weren't cycling, making their own bread and yoghurt and wearing Oxfam shop clothes. This was in sharp contrast to my friends' parents who drove reliable modern cars, ate normal food and bought new clothes. As teenagers, my sisters and I craved some of that normality. We would ask why we couldn't have a modern car that we didn't need to push when it broke down or sliced Hovis bread like our friends. Why were we only allowed tomato ketchup on our birthdays? Their answer was always:

> *Since when did we model our conduct on that of other people?*

My parents didn't want copycat daughters swayed by the values and material possessions of others. I share some of that view, but it's a tough line to hold in our daughters' generation. They are growing up in a world where far more global values and influences are just a mouse-click away, making it even more confusing for them to know who they are and what they should believe in, and what they will resist and what they'll fight for.

I want part of my legacy to my daughters to be that they know their own mind and don't just follow the crowd. I encourage them to be accepting of difference, and I hope they know their views and opinions are welcome, even if we don't agree.

By the way, my daughters loved Granddad's bread and Marmar's Morris Minor.

What are you taking away from the second secret? Make some notes at the back of this book.

Values:

Live by your legacy to your daughter.

REMINDER

Take out of this secret what you feel is right for you and your daughter.

SECRET 3: THE V-SIGNS

KNOW WHAT IS ESSENTIAL TO KEEP YOUR DAUGHTER SAFE AND HAPPY

Discover the secrets of:

- The V-signs - understand the danger zones for girls.
- Virtual - how to cope with technology.
- Violins - managing the pressure points for girls.
- Veruca Salt - dealing with bitches and bullies.
- Vomit and vaginas - how to help her deal with the pleasure and pain of her body.

66 Having a daughter is a joy, but it's also a never-ending list of things for me to worry about. In the early years, I worried about how to keep her alive and even if she wore too much pink. Now she's 14 I still worry about her appearance, but making her safe and happy is what keeps me awake at night. 99

Paul, father of two daughters aged 11 and 14

Parenting a daughter today is difficult and delightful whether she is eight, 18 or 28, judging by what I've learned from the parents I work with. My experience of raising my three daughters and the experiences of all the parents I have interviewed for this book point to serious anxieties about the challenges out there for daughters. Parents at each stage of their daughter's life can be overwhelmed with anxiety. Yet, seeking help (unless it's about how to give birth) can be viewed by yourselves and others, as a sign of being hopeless parents.

Did our parents worry like we do?

In my childhood, I remember my parents worrying about a strange man who loitered in our local park. They also grumbled about how many sweets we ate, saying 'Our teeth would rot'. As teenagers, there were rows about exam results, smoking, unsuitable boyfriends and coming home late. You'll encounter some confessions concerning my teenage naughtiness and anxieties in this chapter, along with some of Marmar's wisdom on how she dealt with us.

Those same worries still persist, but the biggest change for today's parents is technology and its influence on our daughters. I can't imagine how previous generations would have dealt with the radical changes technology has created, and how nimble we now need to be to keep up with its fast-moving pace.

I believe parenting is an art *and* a science. My approach comes from a combination of intuition, experience, books, advice and reflection. This book is in part an attempt to give you ideas and solutions to the day-to-day issues that confront parents while staying true to the values, wisdom and humour of previous generations.

66 *My current challenges are selective deafness, friendship issues, fussy eating and dreadful table manners.* 99

Linda, mum of three daughters
aged five (plus), seven and nine

This chapter is a guide to the main areas that concern parents of daughters, along with ideas of how to cope. Even if you have no particular worries at the moment, I want to encourage you to read on to learn about what might be coming your way! Daughters have also been telling me what worries them - their answers may surprise you.

66 *I worry if I will ever meet Tom Daley.* 99

Polly, aged 12

Do we need to be worried?

66 *I think parents worry that you have, as a parent, not trained her enough for the real world.* 99

Eve, aged ten

Sometimes, our fears for our daughters are real. Perhaps your daughter is struggling at school or with friends, or perhaps she has changed her eating habits. Maybe she is just unhappy and you don't know why, but you live with her pain and anxieties every day.

Sometimes our fears are exaggerated. The media, other parents, family and friends, parenting experts (!) and our own tendency to expect the worst can fuel our fears. However, anxious parents breed anxious daughters. It's important to know the difference between what is current and true, and what is imagined so we can save our energy for something that is really worth worrying about.

I remember listening to a client who could hardly breathe as she rattled off numerous fears she had about her daughter. I asked her to pause, and write down *everything* that was worrying her. After doing that (it was a long list), she scaled her anxieties according to how real they were and how serious they were, and then she could see which ones she really needed to tackle.

Her panic was getting in the way of her being able to focus on what to do, so dealing with the panic was the crucial first step.

> *" As a parent of grown-up daughters as well as youngsters I have worked out that the only way forward in challenging situations is honesty about your own fears for them – the 'why' is the most important thing to explain. "*

Maria, mother of four daughters aged 11, 18, 25 and 27

What are we worried about?

The world can be a scary place where bad stuff happens to hurt our darling daughters. Parents fear the danger of strangers, in the street and online, but anyone can hurt her from family and friends to teachers and others she meets. The media and the Internet will leave her vulnerable to a 24/7 stream of global opinions and the influence of photo-shopped images of stick-thin women. She can also hurt herself.

I asked parents interviewed for this book about their biggest fears. The winners, in order, were:

1. Technology
2. Alcohol, smoking and other drugs
3. Puberty, porn and sex
4. Peer pressure
5. Self-esteem and body image

Here are some of the specific problems parents have raised:

- My daughter is jealous of her sibling – they argue non-stop.
- My daughter only wants Mummy and is horrible to Daddy.
- My daughter is left out of playground games.
- My daughter is teased about her shoes and the contents of her lunchbox.
- My daughter struggles with her homework.
- My daughter texts me to say she's run out of lunch money, again.
- My daughter is miserable because her clothes are too tight, but she loves baking and eating cakes.
- My daughter is losing weight.
- My daughter started her periods – aged nine.
- My daughter is online – I thought she was asleep.
- My daughter's boyfriend dumped her for her 'best' friend.
- My daughter is self-harming.
- My daughter smells of booze and fags.
- My daughter thinks her exam results are a 'disaster'.
- My daughter has no idea how vulnerable she is coming home late, alone and drunk.

These are some of the behaviours and problems that cause parents to worry. I imagine you can add your own worries to this list. Write them down on the notes pages at the back of the book.

> " *Puberty, porn and sex – my No. 1 worries for my daughter.* "

Simon, dad of Helen aged 21

The next step is to attempt to understand the source of a daughter's pain before we can work out how best to help her. We need to see behind the behaviour, to try to stand in her shoes and to imagine what is going on for her. It might not be obvious; perhaps you have a feeling something is not quite right, but I am a great believer in parental intuition.

Be a detective. Pay close attention to what you see, what you hear and what you notice that is different, and then think about how the results of your detective work make you feel. Balance that urge to inspect with the need for your daughter in her teen years to seek privacy.

> " *If I am worried about something embarrassing, my mum can always tell and she has a nice talk with me to sort it out.* "

Jess, aged ten

How is she hurt?

Physically – her body can be criticised, abused or neglected, by others or herself. Growth spurts and puberty can be really painful.

Emotionally – her heart can generate strong feelings such as sadness, jealousy, rage and dissatisfaction. And the first time she falls in love (even if it's with a singer in a band – David Essex as you all know by now in my case), is a gut-wrenching time for her and for her parents.

Mentally – her mind can frighten, confuse and limit her.

Spiritually – she can feel her life has no meaning or purpose. She could also be obsessed by a religion or culture.

These areas often overlap one another. For example, a physical 'hurt', such as spots, also affects emotional and mental well-being. It's hard for parents to know how, or whether, to save our daughter from these hurts or to just accept they are part of growing up. These hurts are a breeding ground for our fears that can produce panic reactions. Saying 'no thanks' to roast potatoes doesn't mean she needs a lecture on a balanced diet or that she is on her way to an eating disorder. The truth is, our understandable need to protect her and fix her pain is a short-term act of care, but a long-term act of disablement. Her self-esteem can plummet when we overprotect her or try to solve her problems for her. There is a new term called 'snowplough parenting', which means that parents are doing everything they can to clear any obstacles that might hurt or impede their child. Helicopter parents have been hovering over daughters for a while, protecting and over managing their darlings.

> " *Don't be scared to let them loose on the world. Don't cottonwool your child because they're female.* "

Jenni Herd, aged 16, who wrote to the editor of *The Times* resenting the media's negative portrayal of teenagers, and calling for them to be respected instead

Your daughter could feel that her efforts at homework, for example, are not good enough. She picks up your fears when you line up tutors and extra work books or finish her homework for her. To your daughter, this can translate into her feeling *she* is not good enough for you. If she experiences nagging, criticism and continual reminders about everything from music practice to bedtimes, she is likely to stop listening, withdraw and feel incapable. In social situations, if we phone ahead to the host of a play date or a sleepover to prepare the way for our daughter by saying she might be shy, does not like tomatoes or will have a meltdown if she loses in a game, how will your daughter ever learn to deal with these things herself? Instead, our daughters thrive when we tool them up, taking into account their age and personality, so they feel capable and good about themselves. I will show you how as this book unfolds.

> *It's tough recognising it's their life, and in the end they must make their own decisions, and that you can't protect them from all pain and disaster. That's tough.*

Esther Rantzen, founder of ChildLine and journalist and TV presenter

If we want our daughters to grow up strong and able to cope with something that hurts her physically, emotionally, mentally or spiritually, the best thing we can do is to:

TIP

Show her how to protect herself.

Parents – you have a great job to do here

You have a vital role to play in helping your daughter learn how to be safe and to feel confident. You have the power to help her feel good about her capabilities to do these things. In part her capability will come from her learning the hard way - by making mistakes, but many daughters I surveyed want just this.

66 *We need to learn from our own mistakes.* 99

Lily, aged 18

I realise this vital role can also sound like a huge responsibility, but you can choose to see this as an opportunity, not as additional pressure or another thing to feel guilty about.

My third secret is: Know what is essential to keep your darling daughter safe and happy. Ignorance is no use to her, or to you. I have written a guide for you, which is intended to have timeless relevance but as new ideas come to light on parenting daughters, I will put them up on www.darlingdaughters.org. The principle behind this guide is to keep an eye out for what *your* daughter is up against. You will find advice and ideas that will help you unpick any 'new' problems and, I hope, ease your worries. And remember, there is specialist help you can turn to. (See the Directory on pages 259–262.)

V is for Virtual

> 66 *She wants a Facebook page and she's only nine. So far, I'm saying 'no', but I'm not sure how long I can hold out.* 99

Parent

I'm starting with 'virtual' because technology is the biggest daily worry for the parents I interviewed, and it still is for me.

The fear of what our daughter is getting up to online via computers and mobile phones can be a panic button for parents. Technology is an unmatched source of learning, information, entertainment and socialising. Your daughter loves using it. Parents love using it too. What else is so immediately gratifying? All her friends are on it, and you are likely to be the meanest parents on the planet if you try to ban or control her usage of it. Losing her phone would be a major catastrophe to your daughter.

> 66 *Mum and Dad are really annoying about my phone. They make me leave it outside my room at night, but I know there are some kids in my class who are gaming all night and they fall asleep at school.* 99

Alice, aged 14

Watching our daughter using technology, (and she's probably far quicker at it than we are) can leave us feeling left out, unsure and worried about what she's being exposed to. I know some parents who have cut plugs off computers, hidden phones and cancelled contracts in desperation to control their daughter's online world.

A parent's story about technology

" I have a daughter aged 14 and a son who is 11. My biggest worry is that she doesn't want to spend time with our family but she goes round to her boyfriend's house all the time, where there are no rules. Added to that she has had some disgusting things posted on Facebook about her and her boyfriend by her so-called 'friends'. Fortunately, my wife is also friends with our daughter's friends on Facebook, so she could see first-hand what was being said about her. My wife just waded in on Facebook, where everyone could see it, and told them to stop putting up all these horrible things about our daughter and to leave her alone. That stopped it, but I think I'll back off a bit too, as nagging her about her boyfriend is getting me nowhere. I'll just keep inviting him round, as his dad isn't on the scene and I think he quite likes it at our place. "

Colin, dad of a daughter aged 14 and a son aged 11

I am including Colin's story because it's an honest account from a dad who was worried about his daughter's relationship that was also the subject of some nasty Facebook posts.

What I particularly like is:

- He admits how hard he finds it that his daughter wants to go to her boyfriend's house where there are no rules.
- His wife took a risk by using Facebook to alert her daughter's friends that their behaviour was unacceptable and had to stop.
- He is prepared to look at his own behaviour and make changes by backing off from nagging, and to keep offering welcoming invitations to the boyfriend.

The reality is our daughters are growing up with technology, and they will be using it forever. My own teenage daughter has never known a world without Internet, email and mobile phones. It's available everywhere via Wi-Fi, and whatever latest networks are on offer. Even when you or her teachers think she is offline, she might not be. As parents, our job is to keep up with what's on offer and to help her use it wisely. If you talk to her about this, even if she rolls her eyes or accuses you of being an interfering dragon, studies show she is *more* likely to stay safe, *more* likely not to arrange to meet strangers and *more* likely not to give out her contact details. I learnt early on not to rely on schools to do all the technology safety teaching for me. Find out what your school teaches and support this with your own conversations. If your school doesn't offer a technology information event, encourage them to set one up.

When your daughter was little, you taught her how to cross the road and use a sharp knife. The value of your time instructing her then has meant she can negotiate a road or use a knife safely without needing you. Teaching her about the safe way to use technology needs the same investment from you. The difference though, is that technology is changing all the time and it's hard to keep up.

We need to keep the right information, our parental controls and our filters up to date. It's really hard and we're all too busy, but I think this deputy head teacher sums this up better than I can:

> **"** *The biggest problem we have in school over technology is that parents don't have a clue what their children are capable of online. They buy them the latest gadget to keep them quiet, but it's like giving them a car without teaching them how to drive it safely.* **"**
>
> Deputy head teacher at a primary school

I am not a technology expert, and to be honest, I find it boring, but I have had to force myself to engage with the enormity of its influence in my daughters' lives. Coming up are some of my favourite tips that have helped me, but it's vital to supplement these tips with your own research.

Parents with older darlings often say to me they wish they had thought more about technology rules when their girls were younger, but that now it feels too late to try to bring in rules and regulations. I understand; it can be hard to suddenly ask your teenage daughter to stop being glued to her mobile, but I want to encourage you to take a fresh look at what's going on and what changes you want to make.

In your family what is allowed, and when? (Jot down your answers on the notes pages at the back of the book.)

Your daughter and devices – tips for parents
1. Work out what kind of technology access she can have, your budget and how much time she is allowed on it.

2. Take her with you to get her phone (or other devices) and let her do most of the talking with the shop assistant so she is very clear about how the phone works, what the deal includes and who is paying. (It's hard to say what is the right age for a first phone, and it will depend on your needs to keep in touch and her ability to be responsible.)

3. Limit time allowed on screens and be clear what the rules are on school days, weekends and holidays.

4. Make meal times screen and phone free.

5. Keep phones and Internet devices out of bedrooms overnight.

6. Tell her you're proud of her when she stays within her time and budget limits.

7. Have a regular 'no screens and phones' day. We found just after Christmas was a good time to try this. My daughters said it was such a relief to be offline for 24 hours that they want to repeat this every school holiday.

How much are *you* online?

> 66 *For me, I work a lot and I take calls on my mobile at all hours. I would like to take less when in my daughter's company. However, that's life and when you do have time for fun, take it!* 99
>
> Mark, dad of a daughter aged seven

Sorry, nobody likes to face up to this one, but how much we're online working, surfing, shopping or socialising is going to affect how much notice our daughter takes of our rules or requests about her own usage.

Tips for parents on their use of devices

Watch your own usage! Are you always on your phone or computer? Show your daughter the value of including other things in your day without being interrupted by phones or emails. Say out loud: 'I'm going to sit down, have a cup of tea and leave my phone on silent in the hall.'

Ask your daughter to help you create your social media account or set up your phone. It will help her self-esteem if she feels she can show you how to do something for a change. As she shows you, you can ask her questions about privacy and security, which could be a productive conversation.

Request to be her friend on social media sites, such as Facebook, but don't be surprised if she blocks you – privacy is part of being a teenager. The suggested age for Facebook is 13, but the reality is many get round this rule by faking their birth date. If she is under 16, she is still a minor and your responsibility. You could insist she can only have an account if you have access to it.

Have fun with her on communication apps such as Snapchat and Whatsapp. We have a family Whatsapp group that means we can share jokes, information and news in seconds – fantastic now we're all miles apart most of the time. Download the free games apps she likes, so you can see the kind of screen time she enjoys and why.

Do things together online, play games, do the supermarket shop, have fun sorting photos, research travel and holiday options or help with homework projects.

What about the telly?

Television is now a 24/7 multi-channel option, unlike in my childhood when we had three channels on a second-hand black and white TV that often went on the blink. On demand TV means the 9.00 p.m. watershed is meaningless. There have been programmes on TV that I believed to be suitable for a 13-year-old, only to find that they contained more violence than one of my daughters could tolerate. I insisted that we changed channels. You know your daughter best.

Tips for parents on TV

What limits are you setting around what programmes are being watched and for how long? Ask your daughter what limits she might suggest. Her answer may surprise you.

Create your own watershed and review it at birthdays and the New Year (or at another break point in the year, such as the summer holidays).

Watch quality programmes together and talk about them. This includes sometimes watching what she wants to watch, without lots of moaning about what a rubbish programme it is. Find out what she likes about it instead.

A TV in a child's bedroom doesn't help them interact with the family, sleep well or help you keep an eye on what they are watching. Interestingly, there has been a 17 per cent drop in this, as children prefer the massive screen in the living room. But if your daughter is allowed a smartphone, tablet or laptop in her own bedroom she can watch anything from the comfort of her cosy bed.

The blue light emitted by screens disturbs the eyes and the brain, preventing good sleep. Studies show that our eyes need at least 30 minutes screen-free before we should attempt to go to sleep.

Do something else instead of TV. Though your daughter is likely to moan or create some excuse for why she has to watch *The Great British Bake Off*, you can still insist that the TV goes off. Try and understand her need to keep up with conversations at school the next day, but help her record whatever she needs to watch and agree a time when she can catch up. As with anything highly addictive and instantly gratifying, distraction helps.

> 66 *Sam is quite strict with the TV. It's not on too much, and doesn't tend to be on in the mornings.* 99

David Cameron, Prime Minister

In the heat of the moment when you have groaned for the umpteenth time at your daughter to find something else to do, keep a few alternative ideas up your sleeve. I love it when I hear about a positive parenting tip, or experience one myself. One family asked their children to write a list of TV alternatives. The title of this list, which lived on the fridge, was:

Screens off; now what?

What to do when it's time to unplug

Here are some more good ideas from parents about what goes on in their family when it's time to unplug. You'll notice that going shopping is not included as a TV alternative.

Use this list and add your own ideas for those times when you need to switch everything off.

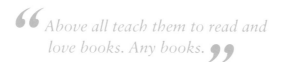

> *Above all teach them to read and love books. Any books.*

Tom, dad of three almost grown-up daughters

Have a conversation. Girls love to chat! Ask for her opinion on anything, including her ideas on what she can do instead of being in front of a screen.

Read a book. Even if it is on an electronic device, and your daughter may be leaping in and out of social media at the same time, she is still reading. Ask her how the book is going and if she would recommend it. Tell her you're happy to see her engaging with a book – be genuine, and don't be put off if she accuses you of being sarcastic. If you're reading a good book, describe to her what you like about it.

Play fight or tickle her.

Be active. Go for a walk, a bike ride or play a sport.

Go out. Visit a library, park, museum or gallery.

Make a mess in the kitchen. Plan and cook a meal, or wash up together.

Pay the family pet some special attention. Walk it, stroke it, play with it or clean out its cage.

Help her tidy out a cupboard in her room, or ask her to help you tidy a cupboard.

Get crafty. Bring out the paints, modelling clay and the craft box.

Play a game - board game, word game, charades, cards - what do you like to play?

Write a letter. Marmar said a handwritten letter was far more appealing and less likely to be thrown away than an email or a text.

Chores for cash. Keep a list of chores you are prepared to pay for, such as spring-cleaning or car washing. (See also the guide to chores on pages 277–279.)

Put on some music and dance.

Stage a bin-liner fashion show. Within half an hour and one bin liner per player and the craft box, everyone in the family has to create an outfit.

Get a makeover. Set up a living room salon and treat each other (dads included) to a manicure, a hand massage or a new hair-do.

You might think that screens off equals initial boredom, which could lead to mischief, but some boredom is important. It enables children to be creative or to try something new. It is not our job to be the sole source of entertainment suggestions or to keep them quiet and 'happy'.

The other truth here is that it has been shown that what children love most is our time. Showing an interest in alternative pursuits is so valuable, even if it doesn't feel like it at the time.

> **❝** *I like it when my dad is supportive of my music and when my mum compliments me and we do stuff together.* **❞**

Issy, aged 14

Setting limits

We can become really fed up with the arguments that are caused when we try to impose limits and the nagging sense of disappointment that our daughter doesn't appear to rate anything unless it involves technology, especially when it's the weekend or a holiday.

I wish this whole business of growing a healthy relationship with technology was easy, but it isn't. When we get angry, nag, give up or offer bribes it doesn't help anyone. It will be easier if you can set clear rules in the first place, and not get sucked in to sessions of moaning and tantrums that occur when it's time to unplug and do something else.

> **❝** *Don't be too soft because then your daughter will think she can get away with anything.* **❞**

Daisy, aged ten

Technology is exciting, fast and addictive. I call it 'digital crack' – you can expect withdrawal to be painful, just as going cold turkey hurts a drug addict. The path out of this is not to offer an alternative 'high' via treats, rewards or incentives. The path out requires you to be strong enough to weather the storm of grumpy daughters.

In time, there is more of a chance that your daughter will experience and appreciate having clear rules and a mum and dad that stick to them. It's one of those parts of being a parent that can be hard work, tedious and infuriating, but your daughter will eventually realise the benefits of having a more rounded approach to how she spends her time. Sometimes, she may surprise you and switch off anyway and find something else to do.

House rules on screen time

When Phoebe, aged 15, was asked what advice she would give to parents bringing up daughters, her answer was: 'Rules'.

Rules set people free. Without clear and simple rules, we create a lot more stress, misunderstandings and arguments for ourselves and for our daughters. With a few clear, positively phrased rules that are agreed, you all have something to refer back to.

If your daughter is under ten, you will do most of the explaining and setting the rules, but of course they need regular updating as children grow older and needs change. It is possible to set rules for the first time even when your children are in their teens.

Five tips to setting some technology house rules

Add to these ideas and jot them down here or on the note pages at the back of the book.

1. School holidays (six times a year in the UK) offer an opportunity to reboot your family rules.

2. Start by having a conversation with your partner (if you have one) so you can be as united as possible on all house rules.

3. Decide who is responsible for maintaining the safety filters on the family's technology.

4. Jointly consider each of your children, their age, their temperament and if they need Internet access for school work. If you're not sure, check with their school.

5. Decide what rules you're both happy with, and crucially which can be realistically enforced. For example, no phones at meal times or all gadgets off by 10.00 p.m.

The American Association of Paediatricians recommends that screen time should be earned; it's not a right. For example, screen time could be earned for completing homework, chores and some reading for pleasure. Comment positively whenever you see your daughter sticking to the rules, but if she doesn't, warn her that you will be taking her phone, laptop or tablet away. Empty threats don't work, so saying 'That's it! No phone for a fortnight' and then giving it back to two days later will mean she knows you will give in.

How on earth will I introduce new rules to my girls, let alone stick to them?

Family meeting

I first came across the idea of a family meeting during my parenting course training. I thought it sounded too formal, but I decided to give it a go and it turned out to be a great way of listening to each other talk through a family decision or a dilemma.

We started off with something light-hearted like 'What shall we do for half term?' but the *process* of the meeting has meant that since then, we have used it as a productive way to sort out more serious issues that affect all of us. If you have never had a family meeting, I suggest you start by having one on a topic that is unlikely to end in an argument. That way, your children will be building up an expectation that family meetings are worthwhile.

Tips for setting up a family meeting

- Let everyone know the time, date and place of the meeting. It could easily coincide with a mealtime. If children younger than ten will be at the meeting, limit the pow-wow to 15 minutes.

- Tell everyone why you want to gather together and express it positively. For example, 'We need to have a chat about what's going on over the festive break.'
- Make sure YOU are feeling robust, fed, watered and calm if you want the meeting to go well.
- Make sure you and your partner know you are sure of your bottom-line position, but be open to all other suggestions and ideas.
- Meeting etiquette could include no technology, only one person speaking at a time and agreeing that no ideas are stupid. You and your family will come up with a host of other ideas.

Thank everyone for his or her attention.

Agree who's taking notes.

Ask for everybody's ideas.

Meeting will end when we have reached an agreement. (For under-tens, you may have to take a lead on the decision taking into account what has been said.)

As with trying anything new, have high hopes and low expectations. It may take a few goes before a family meeting becomes a regular and positive way of resolving family decisions.

> 66 *It was only when we had a family meeting about meal times that my daughter plucked up the courage to say she just couldn't stand anyone farting in the kitchen. Our kitchen is now a fart-free zone!* 99
>
> Julie, mum of three teenage daughters

With potentially tricky issues such as setting new rules about technology with a teenage daughter, you could start by saying, as parents, that you made a mistake by not having clear rules in the first place and that you are no longer prepared to carry on nagging and arguing as it's no good for anyone. Listen to your daughter's ideas about how much screen time she would say is fair.

She may not like the outcome of a meeting. She may feel she is being punished. You can reflect her fury or her irritation using empathy, 'I can see you're fed up with me for taking your phone away. I imagine you wish I wasn't so strict.' She may moan, shout or worse, but if you give in you might have only bought a temporary peace. You may well go through the whole scenario again when you next attempt to put your foot down. Any sign **at all** that she is complying, needs encouragement from you. For example, 'Thank you for remembering to leave your phone on the hall table overnight without me reminding you.'

Technology is a vast subject and it changes constantly with new products and updates for software coming at us all the time. It can feel like a never-ending tsunami. Trying to cover all the best tips in each area of technology would fill the whole chapter.

The one thing that I hope you'll take seriously is that it is *our* job as her parents to be wise not ignorant about technology and how she is using it. I have listed my current favourite websites for specific help and advice in the Directory (page 253). Some websites have really useful age-related checklists of what you need to watch out for and masses of good advice on safety, how to set controls, products and medical information, which will all help your confidence in taking control of technology usage in your home.

Tips on technology safety

I have heard too many parents say: 'I give up on this one, the kids know far more about it than I do.' Just as you wouldn't expect a toddler to teach herself how to cross a road or use a sharp knife, it's our job to know how to teach them to use technology. Here are some helpful tips on safety.

" My 11-year-old was researching a school project about New Zealand. She typed 'Views of New Zealand' into the search engine, and although there were lovely pictures of mountains and sheep, there were also pictures of gay men having sex. "

Jenny, mum of three daughters

- **The Internet can be accessed** everywhere so your daughter needs to know how to keep herself safe online when she's out of reach of the safety filters and time limits that would be installed at home or at school.
- **Discuss, don't lecture**. You could say, 'This is hard for me. Do I put a fence at the top of the cliff or send an ambulance to the bottom of the cliff?' Listen to her ideas.
- **Uploading images** – ask your daughter if she would be happy to parade down the high street in her bikini. If not, then why would she, or allow others to, upload photos of herself wearing very little that could be seen by strangers all over the world?
- **Sexting and revenge porn** – taking sexy photos and misusing them is growing rapidly. I heard recently about the increase in revenge porn. This means putting up provocative and intimate images of an ex-partner on public sites or emailing them to other people. There are measures underway to make this illegal, but in the meantime talk to your daughter about the risks involved in allowing anyone to take sexual photos, even if she believes she is in a loving relationship at the time.
- **Contact details** – make sure she never ever puts her contact details online.

*" I use a different name for Facebook to protect
my identity and any unwanted attention from
strangers, but my real friends know it's me. "*

Lizzie, aged 20

- **Privacy settings** – ask your daughter to show you her phone or tablet's privacy settings. Let her see what a stranger could see on her page.
- **Internet and phone history** – while your daughter is under 16 and under your roof, you have the right to access her online history. You love her and you're paying the bill!

Where can I learn more about digital safety?
Knowing how to keep your daughter safe online is your responsibility while she is under 16 and legally a minor, but you'll be gradually handing over the responsibility of her online safety to her.

There is a great YouTube clip called *Think You Know?* (www. youtube.com/watch?v=lOEV647xDeA). It's shown to children towards the end of primary school, but as a parent there is a lot in it that we can learn too, particularly about privacy settings.

*" Mum and Dad always tell me to get off my
laptop or my phone and I hate how they say 'In my
day we never had this technology.' And they don't
understand what it's like growing up in the generation
of iPhones and Apple technology stuff. "*

Lucy, aged 14

What would Marmar have to say about screens?

As a child growing up in the 1970s, the only screen we had was a basic television with three channels. We would all watch comedy or drama on the 'goggle box' as Marmar called it. There were a lot of laughs over *Fawlty Towers*, *Up Pompeii!* or *Dad's Army*. *Z-Cars* gripped us all, as did *The Forsyte Saga*, and Sunday nights were devoted to *The Brothers*. However, when we were clamouring at Marmar asking to be allowed to watch more of our favourites, such as *Top of The Pops* or *Star Trek*, she would sometimes just say, 'Turn off that goggle box!'

We knew she meant it, she only had to say it once and she didn't yell it or mutter it. There was no negotiation. If only it were that simple now! But what I have found works is to agree, in the first place, what programmes can be watched, what time they start and finish, and how they fit in with the agreed amount of screen time. Sometimes, there might be a case for being allowed to watch a special programme. You could say you want to hear two reasons why you should bend the rules, and be prepared to listen. It's OK to break the rules too sometimes, so long as you are clear about why your daughter can stay up late, for example, to watch the *Strictly Come Dancing* final.

V is for Violins

> *My challenge is watching her succumb to the pressures of being a girl (at times) and trying to help her, guide her into the world where she will one day fit in.*

Hilary, a daughter aged eight and a stepdaughter aged six

Why violins? To me they represent the pressure to succeed. When I was 11, I learnt the violin for a year and it was a disaster. My teacher didn't know the meaning of the word 'encouragement' and used criticism and put downs to spur me on to try harder but I just dissolved into tears. She then told me off for the watermarks my tears caused on the school's violin.

The pressure to play the right notes and be good enough to be entered into the exam was intense. Thankfully, my parents could see I was struggling, so lessons were stopped. For many years, I felt a failure, nowhere near 'good enough'. Subsequently, I have found a way round this by joining a local choir that welcomes anyone. As a parent myself, I have found it difficult to know how much pressure to apply to my daughters, and how much to back off. Amy Chua's book, *Battle Hymn of the Tiger Mother*, (Bloomsbury, 2011) provoked strong views from parents all around the world. I find that my preferred route is to be mindful of the harm that over pressurising from parents can cause when added to the twenty-first-century pressures faced by our daughters everyday.

" *Everything I do is just not good enough for my parents. If I get an A, they want to know why it's not A*. I might as well not bother.* "

Eleanor, aged 14

There are frequent surveys published where grim statistics are evidence of the pressure that is felt by our daughters to be perfect. They feel the pressure to succeed at school, to ace their dance exam, to have the coolest friends and to wear the best outfits on their perfect body with the latest phone glued to one hand.

I remember at around the age of seven becoming aware that my friends were cleverer, prettier or could run faster. I also remember how inadequate I felt. Eating cheered me up. Watching my own daughters growing up and trying to deal with the pressures of being twenty-first century girls has been one of the toughest things I have had to cope with, and I know this is true for so many parents. 'They grow up too soon, what's happened to their childhood?' is a common complaint on my courses. As this mum says:

" *Don't let her grow up too fast! Mine wanted a bra recently (she is nearly nine)! I compromised with a cropped vest (which I still don't like but it makes her feel a bit more grown up.)* "

Claire, mum of a daughter aged nine

For those girls who feel that they don't meet their parents', their friends' or their own expectations, the unhappiness it creates can be untold. In some instances, it can slide into self-harm. Self-harm covers a multitude of behaviours: not just self-mutilation, but alcohol and other drug abuse and negative self-talk. It's not just teenage girls – younger girls are increasingly worried about their looks, their friends and whether they are 'cool' or not.

" *My friend looks skinny in shorts and I look fat.* **"**

Sophie, aged eight

Self-esteem

All this pressure can seriously harm our daughters' self-esteem. They can feel very low and lack confidence, which can lead to withdrawal, difficult behaviour and self-harm. Self-esteem can blow up and down, especially during the hormone havoc of adolescence. Girls are naturally more sensitive than boys, and they can interpret the slightest telling off or disapproving look as a huge personal insult, which dents their confidence.

One thing that can make an instant difference is recognising that there is no substitute for giving your *time* to your daughter. I remember looking forward to a celebration dinner with old friends one night, but when my daughter came back from school she had clearly had a difficult day. I knew instinctively I should stay at home and cancel the babysitter. It wasn't an easy decision, but it was the right one. Freeing up the evening and hanging around at home, meant we watched some TV, had an omelette together and a good chat about her troubles.

It's not always possible, but if you can free up some time you'll have a better chance of detecting if your daughter's going through a rough patch or if there is something more serious going on. Best of all, by spending time with her, she'll feel loved and cared for, and maybe you will feel less parental guilt.

> *Spend time with your daughter and if she wants to talk to you, create time so that you can talk privately, without siblings or random relatives or other people being there.*

Lara, aged 14

Who is putting this pressure on your daughter?

Other people
Parents, siblings, friends, teachers, family members and other significant adults apply pressure when they are negative, critical or use labels, such as: 'You're a little madam' or 'Your brother is the smart one.'

She does
Our daughters put pressure on themselves by looking at images online or in magazines of models and celebrities. They compare their looks, school grades, 'hotness', sportiness, musicality or anything else to their friends'.

The media
The Internet, magazines, TV, adverts and movies all promote airbrushed images of girls looking beautiful, thin and sexy wearing the right fashion brands.

Social media
A world where everyone else seems to have more friends, a prettier profile picture, funnier posts, a greater volume of re-tweeted Tweets

and more 'likes' on Instagram, blog or Tumblr. Your daughter needs to be fairly thick-skinned and well adjusted to deal with the feelings these can produce.

As parents, we have a crucial job to do here – more than anything or anyone else – to build her self-esteem so she feels loved and lovable.

How do we build our daughter's self-esteem and take the pressure off?

Coming up are some of my favourite ideas to boost self-esteem. There are more that are specifically for mums or dads in Secret 4 (pages 164–184) and Secret 5 (pages 185–205).

TIP

Listen, listen, listen.

66 *Walking... anywhere... they talk you listen, you talk they listen... Things happen on the way that need discussion... and there's time just to be silent together.* 99

Ali Hewson, business owner, mother of two daughters and two sons, married to U2's singer, Bono

By what we say

The power of our words lasts a lifetime. Think about what you can recall your parents saying to you. We usually find it easier to remember the negative stuff that was said, or shouted, in anger or criticism. Our words have great currency, so we need to spend them wisely.

Do whatever it takes to stay calm and to avoid shouting, criticising, blaming, moaning and whining! Daughters can be so sensitive and they need to hear specific praise, even for simple gestures like: 'Thanks for giving me a hug.'

None of us are saints. Sometimes you will revert to being a shouter or a critic, but when you do, make sure you apologise for your behaviour. Later, you could offer a reason for your behaviour, such as tiredness or a difficult day. But avoid saying something to her along the lines of: 'If you had done what I had asked in the first place, I wouldn't have shouted at you.' That issue is a very separate conversation.

Communication tips that will help, not harm, your relationship with your daughter

> " *I don't like it when my mummy calls me silly names.* "
>
> Maddie, aged seven

• Labels

Over time single word labels, such as 'She's so selfish' or 'She's such a stunner', stick, and become self-fulfilling especially when said or written by powerful parents or other significant adults.

Instead of labelling your daughter, focus on the effort she is making. Watch out for words that may make her feel that she is failing to live up to a certain standard, or comparing her to others in the family.

Instead of 'Stop interrupting. Why can't you be polite like your sister?', try 'I want you to wait until I have finished speaking before you speak.'

Don't trap her into traditional girls' activities or the 'girlie' position in the family. Instead of 'You won't want to come to the football with your brother', try 'Who wants to come to the football?'

Self-esteem is very volatile – someone once told me that we need ten hugs a day. This includes physical hugs, but also those moments where we communicate with words and actions our faith, love and pride in our daughter.

• **Describe what you admire and like about her**, often. Instead of saying something general such as 'You're so helpful,' be more specific: 'It was lovely watching you help that toddler on the slide.' Or instead of 'You're such a stunner,' describe what you see: 'That top really brings out the colour of your eyes.'

• **Swap negative labels** for clear questions that give you and her something to aim for. Instead of 'You're so lazy, you're never ready in time for the school bus,' try 'What time do you need to be ready to catch the bus to school?'

• **Ask what she needs from you**. Instead of 'I have told you three times to come and do your violin practice, your exam is tomorrow!' try 'With your exam tomorrow, I don't want my nagging to make you fed up, so I would like to know what are your plans are for your violin practice and what kind of help you need from me.'

• Even **positive labels** can be difficult to live up to. 'Judy is the cheerful one' became a pressure on me to be cheerful or to make my parents laugh.

• **Talk up effort, not results**. Instead of 'Not bad, but you have a long way to go before the exam,' try 'You played that piece several times and I can hear the difference already. Well done.'

> 66 *I can't remember my parents ever shouting. Their first reaction was never to tell us off for doing something, but to wonder why we wanted to do it in the first place.* 99

Hugh Dennis, dad of teenage son and
daughter, actor and comedian, who played
Dad in the family sitcom *Outnumbered*

• **Say very little** – if you're not sure what to say, stay silent. (See How to learn to listen, on pages 274-276.)

> **"** *I have found shutting up instead of waiting for the first opportunity to jump in with advice has been so helpful. My daughter talks to me more now.* **"**
>
> David, dad of Rosie aged seven

• **Name her feelings** as this will help her to handle mistakes. Let the tears flow before you ask what she might do another time, for example: 'I can see how sad you are. When you're ready we can talk about it if you like.'

• Model to your daughter how **you deal with your feelings** or failures by saying it not just thinking it, for example: 'I'm disappointed I didn't get that job after all the work I put into the application. I think I'll phone them and ask for some feedback,' or 'I made a mistake staying up to watch the end of that film. I just couldn't concentrate at work this afternoon.'

You could mention how getting some fresh air or exercise or an early night help you feel better. Sounds obvious maybe, or common sense, but so long as you're not lecturing her, then any of this might help her too.

• **Follow her passions, not yours**, aiming to be open and non-judgemental about her interests. If you criticise her she might give up on a pursuit too easily. Instead of 'What! There's no way you're going to be an actress. I've always said you would make a great teacher,' try 'I agree it's important to find something to do that you are really passionate about and I guess you know acting can be a tough career choice.'

- Offer a positive comment when your daughter does or says something that shows **she knows her own mind**, and that she doesn't just want to follow the crowd. For example you could say, 'I'm impressed that you didn't go to the sleepover because you had your taekwondo exam.'

What you can do to help your daughter feel good about herself

Actions speak louder than words.

> 66 *I want to thank my parents for their unrelenting ability to see the best in me no matter what my track record would suggest.* 99

Harriet, aged 21

- **Believe in her** – have faith that she can make good choices because you have passed on the right morals to guide her. Trust that she will be OK even if she has to learn by her mistakes.
- **Don't hurt her** – make it your aim not to hit, shout or criticise her.
- **Sit down together** – when you both return home, talk about each other's day. It will relax you and send your daughter a message that you're interested in listening.
- **Body language** – keep arms open, relaxed and unfolded.
- **Hugs and kisses** – easier when they're little, but a hug, pat on the back, holding hands or stroking her hair are ways to show you care. Don't worry if she shrugs off your contact during her teens saying, 'Get off!'
- **Distraction** – a little darling under five years old is quite likely to get over minor upsets if you distract her with your enthusiasm for

something else, such as a quick game or a song. I met a parent who would distract her daughter by slipping out and ringing the front door bell! Distraction can remain in your toolkit for older darlings too.

- **Be available –** she might not thank you at the time, but your presence and availability is pure gold. If you say you're too busy to do something with her or to listen to her, she could assume she is boring.
- **Who or what helps you?** Think about who or what helped you as a child when you were upset, feeling a bit low or had a problem. If you can't remember – what helps you now?
- **See her as an individual,** not just in comparison to her siblings. If you find yourself comparing, imagine she was your only child – how would that change your thoughts and behaviour towards her?

66 *They are always there when I need advice, or more importantly – a hug.* 99

Leeanne, aged ten

- **Smile and laugh more**, they just love it and it helps you relax and enjoy each other's company.

66 *My mum makes me happy just 'cos she's so funny.* 99

Jade, aged 21

On a serious note, mental health issues can be easy to misdiagnose by over or under reacting to what you observe in your daughter's behaviour. I am a great believer in parental instinct like this mum:

" Use your own instinct, don't read too much about parenting or be pressurised by family/friends. "

Jan, mum of two daughters aged 13 and 15

Add to these ideas for boosting your daughter's self-esteem on the notes pages at the end of the book.

You know your daughter best. If you're not sure what is wrong with her, or worried, seek support and advice from trusted family and friends, her school, your GP and the contacts and resources listed in the Directory (see pages 253–265.)

What would Marmar say or do about coping with the pressures of growing up?

" If I got upset when Marmar was looking after me, she would say, 'Go and clean your teeth'. "

Marie, Marmar's eldest grandchild

Marmar was a great believer in finding a distraction that could help – little darlings, especially – move on from a problem. I watched her do this many times when my own daughters were young. If they were getting out of hand, squabbling or whining, she would calmly find them something else to do or would make a joke out of it by winking at them and saying:

" Stop it at once, or I'll put you in the bin! "

Marmar

When my sisters and I were teenagers, Marmar definitely found it harder to manage our mood swings or challenging behaviour. She was a night owl, and I know we had some of our best chats 'burning the midnight oil' in the kitchen long after my dad had gone to bed. I can still picture her, wrapped in her coat (she always felt the cold), and brewing tea and eating digestive biscuits and cheese. She was never in any rush to send me to bed if she thought there was more I needed to say.

I can't quite put my finger on why, but I know she believed in us. Maybe it was because she was always pleased to see us. Her face would light up. That devotion helped us to feel loved and capable, and it is something that I aspire to pass on to my own daughters.

V is for Veruca Salt
Bitches and bullies that our darlings have to deal with

"It started when I was about seven and my friends were mean about my tuna sandwiches. Now it's constant little digs about what I look like, my handwriting or what I'm doing at the weekend. I just want it to stop."

Lizzie, aged 13

Friends are a big part of a daughter's daily life. Friendships can last a lifetime. Last night, my friend came round and we spent four hours chatting non-stop about family, work, the menopause, marriage, politics, food and drink, other friends, telly programmes and how many grey hairs we have. We have been friends since we were seven and we're now in our fifties. At Christmas time when all the family is gathered at home, I love seeing my grown-up girls heading out to the pub to catch up with their old childhood friends to talk about how their lives are unfolding now that they're in their twenties.

Friends can also be a source of pain and anxiety. How to deal with friends who are unkind, jealous or bullies is a life-long skill our daughters need. I name these mean girls 'Veruca Salt' after the manipulative character in Roald Dahl's *Charlie and the Chocolate Factory*.

In my youth, friends could be mean to your face or whisper behind your back. I experienced 'friends' calling me names, ridiculing my looks, my outfits, my family and my home. My daughters have all experienced this too, but with the added nightmare of technology sometimes being the messenger for these teasing and hurtful messages. All too frequently, I read about another girl who has committed suicide as a result of being bullied, online and in person.

Daughters are experiencing unprecedented levels of ridicule and rejection as pictures or comments about them are posted to a global audience. This is devastating for them, and made worse in adolescence when they care deeply about their friends' opinions. But when our daughters can develop enough resilience to rise above the words and the actions of these mean girls (or boys) they can save themselves from further harm and, better still, feel stronger and more comfortable in their own skin.

> " I was the girl who was always the first person to put her hand up in class, and it's often not cool to be the person that puts themselves out there, and I was often teased mercilessly. But I found that ultimately, if you truly put your heart into what you believe in, even if it makes you vulnerable, amazing things can, and will happen. "

Emma Watson, actor

As parents, it's hard to know how best to help your daughter deal with the difficulties friendships can cause. Do we interfere, and if so when and how? Should we talk to the 'friend' or contact their parents to let them know their child is being mean?

> " Girls can be so cruel and bitchy, so helping her [our daughter] deal with peers and friendships can be frustrating to both her and me. "

Jackie, mum of a daughter aged eight

Parents - your job is to help your daughter understand the qualities of a good friend, and to learn how to cope when friends turn nasty
Yes, but how? What is a perfect friend? Sadly, he or she doesn't exist, but it's never too soon to talk to your daughter about the kindness and consideration, as well as the shared interests, you would find in a decent friend.

> 66 *Everybody who comes into this building is taken seriously.* 99

Dr Rowan Williams, former Archbishop of Canterbury

Here, Dr Williams was referring to a church that has a particular emphasis on supporting marginalised people, but I like to put this idea into action in our own home.

Be warm and welcoming to friends

As a child, you develop a growing awareness of how your parents view your friends. Whether it's outright judgement, criticism or subtle digs, we don't have to do or say much in order for our sensitive daughters to sense disapproval of her friends.

> 66 *I was about ten, and I remember telling my dad about my friend's parents supporting the miner's strike and he said, 'Her parents would do that – they're Labour voters.' It left me feeling confused but aware that my dad somehow disapproved of my best friend's parents.* 99

Cathy, a parent

Friends - general tips

66 Friends – they're with you when you're laughing, when you're crying, when you're singing, when you're sighing. 99

'Friends', a song by Angela Reith, composer and musical director

- **Talk about the qualities of a decent friend** - acceptance, non-judgemental, loyal, supportive, kind, generous, respectful, considerate - and ask your daughter what she thinks are the qualities of friendship. Boyfriends need these qualities too, and this will be expanded further on pages 180–181 and in Secret 4 (pages 164–184).
- **Be nice to your own friends!** Aim to not say things about other people that you wouldn't be willing to say to their face.
- **Be welcoming and accepting of her friends**, but don't try and be their friend too.
- **Make it easy** for her to bring friends home. Offering hot chocolate and toast was well received on cold days after school.
- Check that **your daughter will explain your house rules** to her friends. It's fine to be both firm and friendly under your own roof, so let visitors know, for example, that phones are turned off overnight and that everyone eats together.
- **Out with friends?** In the excitement of a group of girls getting ready to go out, you may have to take your daughter to one side to make sure you know her plans. Check how she is getting home, what time and with whom.

> *Be the parent who picks up your daughter at the end of an evening. That way you get to see what's going on, who she is with – and it puts a break on alcohol consumption if she knows you will be waiting for her.*

Hilary, mum of two daughters aged 18 and 21

Support team? You might need to be prepared, which includes not being over the drink-drive limit, to go out in your dressing gown at 2.00 a.m. to collect your daughter from a sleepover or from town if she missed the last bus. We tried various ways to keep in touch with our teenage daughters when they were staying out late socialising or babysitting. I couldn't stay awake until the early hours, but I know some parents can't sleep until their daughter is home. In the end, what worked was agreeing that either my husband or I would keep a phone on while they were out and that our daughters would whisper 'good night' so we knew they were home safely.

What to do about mean girls

> *Teach daughters how to stand up for themselves, and how to deal with men.*

Laura, aged 24

Bullying is a big word that creates big waves. It could be describing a serious persistent verbal and/or physical abusive relationship, but it can be a word that is used too liberally for what could be described as minor tiffs. You might be upset by the way your daughter's friends are treating your daughter, but perhaps she is fine and able to brush it off. Compliment her on being strong enough to not let her friends upset her, and at the same time keep a close eye on your daughter for behavioural changes. Clues that she might be experiencing bullying are a marked change in regular behaviour, such as eating or sleeping; tears; difficult behaviour; signs of self-harm; refusing to go to school; broken or missing possessions; or bed-wetting.

Tips for parents on dealing with mean friends

- **Get advice on what to do** - phone a helpline, look online or talk it through with trusted family or friends. Be aware that this episode may remind you of some personal painful experiences, so take care of your own feelings.
- **Take your daughter's feelings seriously** - don't minimise or ridicule what she is saying.
- **Listen forensically** to what she is saying, or trying to say, about how her friends are treating her. She might be finding it very hard to tell you clearly what's going on if she thinks you won't want to hear it, or it will upset you. Good listening without interruption or judgement will help her tell the whole story and may even help her come to her own conclusions. (See How to learn to listen, on pages 274-276.)
- Help your daughter to develop a wide **range of friends** from various sources, such as school, neighbours, clubs or religious groups.

66 *My school mates were being so horrible, but the girls at my dance class are so lovely.* 99

Emily, aged 14

- **Check your school's anti-bullying policy** and be persistent with the school authorities if you feel they're not taking you seriously. Find out about the school's complaints procedure. If you go straight to the head teacher, you might be told that you should have gone to your daughter's head of year first.
- **Contacting the bully's parents** – you may have to talk with other parents about their daughter's behaviour for the sake of your daughter's happiness. Arrange to meet on neutral ground if possible.

  Get the facts right and stick to the evidence without adding your own opinion. Be willing to listen to their side too.
- **What if your daughter is accused of bullying?** Be prepared to listen to the evidence on both sides. You may have to insist that your daughter apologises for being the perceived cause of unhappiness, even if it's not cut and dried or if your daughter thinks it's grossly unfair. Commend her for being willing to own up for her part in causing any unhappiness, and also for apologising.
- **Don't tolerate bullying between family members** – teasing from siblings can turn nasty. I have done all of these things in anger myself, but the truth remains that parents who shout, humiliate, compare and criticise could be misusing their parental power.
- Talk to your daughter about online **privacy settings** and also about how to report cyber bullying and sexting, (which is suggestive images being texted).
- Show your daughter how to put 'In Case of Emergency' (ICE) numbers on her mobile, such as 'ICE MUM' or 'ICE HOME' as UK emergency services are trained to locate these numbers on phones. She can also show the ICE numbers to her friends in case they need to contact you.
- Ask for some of her friends' numbers too so you can ring round to find her!

What would Marmar do or say about mean friends?

" Oh, take no notice of her. "

I have used this expression myself as sometimes it helps to be reminded not to waste time and energy cross-examining everything that our friends say or do which we don't like.

Marmar was always welcoming to any friends we brought home. She was always happy to chat and offer cups of tea to our friends at all hours. They loved her, and as one friend said:

" She [Marmar] was such a laugh! I can see her now, eyes screwed tight and hear that hissing giggle. "

Kitty Taylor

V is for vomit and vaginas

Your daughter's body and how she treats it

From Calpol days and nits, to spots, period pains and her first hangover, sometimes a daughter's body will be a painful place. It's not all bad; a young woman's body can serve her well on the sports field, the dance floor, in the arms of a loving partner and as the cosy and nourishing cocoon in which to grow and deliver a baby.

If you can get your head round the fact that it's your daughter we're talking about, I hope you would agree you would want her to enjoy a healthy sex life when the time is right.

You are probably well aware that she may put her body through hell. In researching this book, I was alarmed to read of cases of anorexia nervosa have been recorded among girls as young as six.

As a mum, I have struggled with the growing popularity of pre-drinks or 'prinks' (or pre-lashing or pre-loading). This is when girls (or boys) pour vast quantities of cheap booze down their slender throats before going out, to reduce their pub or club drinks' bill.

There are so many statistics, surveys and media stories to remind us of what's out there to tempt or harm our daughter's bodies. I don't think you need these hard facts repeated or added to here.

If we want our daughters to grow up without an eating disorder or a body covered in cutting scars, and not addicted to booze, fags or illegal substances then we need to support and guide her on how to self-regulate and to look after her own body.

We want her to recognise when she feels a growing urge to use a coping mechanism - like alcohol or other drugs or thoughtless sex - to deal with short-term difficulties that can could, in fact, cause long-term damage. It is also a normal part of adolescence to show an interest in experimentation and rebellion. But when does 'normal' become worrying? You know your daughter best, so what might be examples of more extreme behaviour need to be relevant to her, and your parental values. Check the list below – it is not meant to frighten you, but to raise awareness of what your daughter could encounter.

What parents need to watch out for:

Changes in eating habits

- Avoiding family meals, dieting or cutting out food groups, such as carbohydrates.
- Calorie counting.
- Eating too much or too little for her weight/age/height. (There is an NHS body mass indicator(BMI) calculator at www.nhs.uk/Tools/Pages/Healthyweightcalculator)
- Binge eating followed by vomiting. (You might hear your daughter vomiting, or smell it.)
- Eating junk food and too much salt and sugar. When it came to crisps, I used to say to my daughters, 'They're just a cold portion of chips. Is it OK to give your body chips every day?'

Fags, booze and other drugs

- Is she experimenting by having a cigarette or on her way to addiction?
- Is she drinking too much or too regularly? As a teenager, you may have drunk beer or cider, but today's teens also buy cheap spirits and mix them with soft drinks to disguise the taste of the alcohol.
- What is your daughter saying about alcohol? For example, has she mentioned comments on needing alcohol in order to enjoy herself or to cope with a problem or difficulty?
- Becoming reliant on painkillers.
- As parents, please be aware of what illegal drugs and legal highs are out there, what they are called and what their effects are. (See the Directory on pages 261–262.)

Her appearance and body
- Sudden weight gain or loss.
- Is she obsessed with exercise or keen to avoid it?
- Has your daughter taken an increased interest – for example, constantly looking in mirrors – in how she looks?
- Wearing baggy clothes to hide weight loss or gain or an image issue, such as persistent negative comments about her image.
- Signs of cuts or burns if she is self-harming. She will conceal these under clothing, so be aware of inappropriate or unusual clothing choices and a reticence to show arms or other parts of her body.
- Skin problems that are causing self-esteem and confidence issues.

(For information on sex and sexuality in relation to this topic, go to pages 155–159.)

I wish I didn't have to write a tip list like that. Perhaps your daughter is fine so far, and will stay that way as she grows up, but she may change, or have friends who are abusing their bodies. Parents I work with have found that it helps to be realistic and informed about the causes, signs and solutions of what their daughter may experience or witness. There may be no quick and easy answers to any of these body issues, but the key point is: if you are at all concerned, take action. Parents who have battled any of these issues say it left them feeling frightened, isolated, guilty and confused about what to do. Friends and family can be helpful and supportive, but also judgemental or dismissive. Start with your GP or school support worker. Look up the websites in the Directory (see page 253) or visit www.darlingdaughters.org.

Facing serious concerns alone makes it twice as hard. If you can, develop a support network for yourself. You don't need a large circle of friends, just one or two people who will listen to you. You can ask for this support by saying something like: 'What would help me the most is if you just listen, so I can get this off my chest.'

What else can parents do to help their daughter protect and enjoy her body?

" I want to thank my mum and dad for making us have dinner all together. "

Lily, aged 17

Food and mealtime tips

My three favourite tips for food and eating problems are:

Eating together at least once a day if possible. Make mealtimes for eating and talking, with phones and TVs turned off. (Jamie Oliver once said the odd meal in front of the TV should be a treat.) Encourage your daughter to help plan, shop and cook meals, not just cupcakes.

Aim to make mealtimes pleasurable rather than an opportunity to lecture or criticise.

Aim to cook the same meal for everyone. One of my family is Coeliac (gluten free) so I fully appreciate the need to cater for special diets, but what has helped is to, where possible, cook the same thing for everyone. Offering an alternative to food that is rejected is the path to growing a fussy eater.

If you already have a fussy eater (sorry about the label!) it doesn't mean she will stay that way. The truth is, it will take effort and determination to get beyond the whinging or refusal to eat a balanced diet. Look at what your daughter eats over a period of three days, instead of panicking if she doesn't eat anything healthy for one day.

A few dislikes can be accommodated, but mealtimes become a nightmare with parents in a flap cooking different foods, at different times for one or more child. Imagine what mealtimes would be like if you didn't have to do that? If your ultimate goal is to help your daughter enjoy a wide range of foods and to be a pleasure, not a pain at mealtimes at home or out, you need to rethink your approach for her benefit and yours.

If possible, try to take a relaxed approach and cook the same food for everyone, and eat it yourself. Children are sometimes simply not hungry enough at mealtimes, but there's more chance of them eating if they have not had anything (except water) for two hours before a meal. It's tempting to give in to pleading looks and cries of 'I'm hungry,' but if you want to break the cycle of fussy eating, stop giving snacks. Any sign of an improved diet or of trying new foods should be cheered!

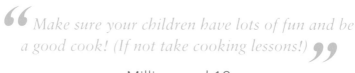

Make sure your children have lots of fun and be a good cook! (If not take cooking lessons!)

Millie, aged 12

More tips about food and eating

• **Share out the meal planning**, shopping, cooking, eating and clearing up. From around aged two, your little darling is able to pick items off supermarket shelves and load them into a trolley, take a dish to the sink and peel fruit and vegetables. By the time she leaves primary school, how about cooking one meal a week?

• **Teach your daughter to cook.** The following framework will help you pass on any skill, not just cooking.

I show her how to chop a carrot.
We do it together.
You let her do it.

• **Carry on offering** foods that they have rejected. It may take a while, but persist. I didn't like Marmar's favourite mushrooms until I was in my thirties.

• **Be creative** with blending vegetables into soups or pasta sauces. A mum I heard about told her daughter that carrot sticks were 'orange chips'.

• **Tap water on the table** with every meal, including breakfast.

• **Don't label mealtime or diet behaviour.** Comments like: she's greedy or too fat or too skinny or too fussy can seriously affect your daughter's relationship with food. Instead, try saying something like, 'Two biscuits is enough' or 'Shall we share the last sausage?'

• **Avoid talking about diets**, cutting out food groups or calorie counting.

Don't criticise your own body as being fat, thin or wrinkly. It's normal to like some parts of our body and not be so keen on other parts, but emphasise health and energy as being the main reason to think about what you put into your body.

> *" PLEASE mothers... don't discuss your own dieting and weight issues with your daughters! If you lose a few pounds, keep it to yourself. If you put on a few pounds, keep it to yourself. Your vulnerable daughters do not need to know! "*

Sue, now grown up, remembering her mum's attitude to weight

• **Talk about nutrition** and which foods keep you well and give you energy, glowing skin and healthy hair.

• **Changes in her eating habits**? It may be a phase or it could be the beginnings of an eating disorder. Don't panic, but do seek help from websites recommended in the Directory (see page 253) or by your GP.

• **Celebrate the delights of food**. Let your daughter see you enjoying all kinds of foods, eating chocolate or having a pudding. Don't take the joy out of celebrations by over-policing portion sizes or by making comments about too much sugar.

• **Make your daughter her favourite meal on her birthday**. On exam days, make her a special treat, like pancakes for her breakfast.

" Eat as a family as often as possible. Tasty food, endless patience, and lots of chips. And if you prepared the meal – you don't wash up. "

Simon Mayo, radio presenter and author, dad of a grown-up son and daughter and a teenage son

Fags, booze and other drugs

Aged 13, my friends and I were smokers of menthol cigarettes, bought by older friends and smoked out of bedroom windows or at the park. I was fortunate enough not to become addicted to cigarettes, but some of my friends did. The same was true about alcohol and cannabis, and sadly, some friends developed serious addiction levels. Teenage experimentation is a normal stage of development, but as parents, we can help our daughters to know when to say no.

Be pro-active and make it your business to know what is available and its effects. Drugs often have nicknames, such as 'charlie' for cocaine, and it's hard to keep up with the multiple names given to the substances available. I thought I had a fairly good understanding of drugs until I went to the drugs talk at my daughter's school.

Tips for you (Sorry if these sound bossy.)

Don't smoke – the health risks are well known. It turns teeth yellow and your body smells like an ashtray. If you smoke, you'll struggle to chase after your grandchildren, if you live that long.

Don't take illegal drugs and watch out how much you depend on painkillers and energy drinks. Before reaching for the headache pills, take a walk in the fresh air and drink plenty of water.

Alcohol is a tough one. It's become socially acceptable, relatively cheap and easily available. Girls vary hugely in height and body mass, and the smaller they are the less alcohol their body can take. In the UK, according to the National Association for Children of Alcoholics, one in five children are affected by their parents' drinking. We may need to be prepared to curb our own drinking habits in order to help educate our daughters. There, I've said it.

If you're in the habit of drinking every day, set aside days where you don't drink. At least two alcohol-free days a week are recommended.

Role model your own management of alcohol. 'I'd love a beer, but it's my turn to drive.'

Talk about the alcohol content of drinks. Better still demonstrate the percentages of alcohol in spirits compared to beer or wine by asking your daughter to measure out the units using water.

Be honest if there are alcohol or other drug problems within the family. A tendency to misuse or develop an addiction can have genetic links.

If your daughter's drunk or high, don't get into an argument but make sure she's safe, any vomiting has ceased, and she has water. Talk about your concerns when she's sober and you are calm.

Your body, her body

" I know my parents worry I'm being influenced in the wrong way by other people and the media, things like body image and drugs/drinking. "

Hayley, aged 17

I hate gyms, but when I turned 50 it occurred to me that it might be a good idea to move a bit more and strengthen my asthmatic lungs. I bought a pair of trainers and took up running. It was awful to begin with, sometimes still is, but I have just completed a ten-kilometre run for charity. I love how much energy regular running gives me. I am a fan of dogs, and our dog has been brilliant for our girls in their teen years, but a brisk walk several times a week without a dog is just as good, especially if you have a desk job.

If you can get outdoors with your daughter it creates time and space in which to chat, or share a run, but don't use it as a chance to lecture her if you want her to come out with you more often.

Other issues relating to your daughter and her body, might be found from page 40.

Piercings and tattoos
I have come to the conclusion that this is an area of cultural influence and of daughters asserting their independent identity. It's an area I find difficult as I can't stand needles and don't like looking at metal on faces. I am fine, though, with bits of metal in ears. Guess that just means I'm old fashioned and hypocritical! By law in the UK, no child under the age of 18 can have a tattoo. Currently, there is no lower age limit on piercings.

Tattoos are much more painful, difficult and expensive to remove than a piercing. If you really struggle to accept tattoos, talk with your daughter about tattoos when she's in her prom dress, at a job interview, in her wedding dress and when she is much older. What will a tattoo of her current boyfriend's name mean when she's forty? Apparently President Barack Obama has so far put his daughters off tattoos by telling them that if they get a tattoo, he will get an identical one in the same place on his body. Piercings may be a problem for you, but banning them could mean that your daughter comes home looking like a pincushion the minute she gets the chance. I insisted on taking my daughters to reputable ear piercing salons where good advice was provided on aftercare.

What would Marmar do?

> 66 Me, aged 13: *'Can I get my ears pierced?'*
> Marmar: *'No, you have enough holes in your body without making any more.* 99

Marmar's answer did give me a quip that I could throw back to my friends when they were having a go at me for still wearing clip-on earrings. I had to wait until I was 18 before I got my ears pierced, and Marmar was still not happy about it.

Marmar was delightfully uninterested in fashion, hair, make-up or appearances, although she did know how to dress up for special occasions. She belonged to an era when powder and lipstick, applied in seconds, and perfume – just a dab behind the ears and on the wrists – was all that was needed. I can recall Marmar smelling special and associating it with a goodnight kiss before she went out. When my own daughters were little, I got into the habit of leaving a lipstick kiss imprinted on their hands before I went out as a playful mark of comfort and care – they loved it – they tell me they still do.

Body tips for you
• **Don't moan** about your own wobbly bits or wish you looked younger. Instead use words like fit and healthy rather than fat and thin. If you need to address your own weight issue, talk about the health benefits it will bring, such as more energy and strengthened heart and bones.

• Talk about and show your daughter examples of **'before' and 'after' photos** that demonstrate the falsehood created by airbrushing and image software.

• **Listen to your daughter** if she is talking about her body and being critical. If she says, 'I'm fat', it's tempting to say 'No you're not!' but it will help her more if you reflect it back, 'You think you're fat?' Ask her what prompted her to think this. The notion may have been planted by friends being unkind or talking about themselves and their body image or your daughter may be comparing herself to images or friends. Use empathy: 'I guess it's hard for you to think you're fat.'

• You could also **offer information** on what she needs to be eating at her age. For example, an overweight teenager and her mum were greatly helped by a visit to a nutritionist. It could be equally useful to your daughter to have an independent person talk about what to eat, portion size, ratios of food groups and to suggest recipes, which would work for all the family, that increase energy and have huge health benefits.

• **Cook together and** experiment with foods, recipes and new tastes. It can take more than 15 tastes of a food to like it. There's still hope for the Brussels sprout!

• Aim to help her get **the right amount of sleep for her.** Use age as a guideline, but some kids need more sleep than others. Support a sound night's sleep with a relaxing bedtime routine that could include a bath, a story or reading time; and excludes TVs or other screens in the bedroom. Lie down with your daughter for a few minutes of peace or a quiet chat. I still do this with my grown-up darlings. Obviously, sleep deprivation will damage your daughter's ability to thrive during the day and will make her more of a handful for you and her teachers. (See the Directory for more sleep ideas on pages 253–265.)

• **Support any interest she shows in sports.** Encourage her to walk, cycle, run to the park, swim, scoot, rollerblade – anything to get her moving.

• **Get a dog** or borrow one if you can. We were advised that it was better for the dog to belong to the whole family, not just to one person. On a dog walk, you can have a great chat, mull over things or just stroll in silence.

• If you're are doing the **school run** by car, park your car as far from the school as feasible and walk the last bit together. Do the same if using public transport to get your daughter to school – see if you can get off one stop early? After a bit of exercise, your daughter is more likely to arrive at the school gate in a better mood and ready to learn.

• **Mirror, mirror on the wall** – girls like to look in them a lot, do you? Show her, especially mums, that it's OK to leave the house minus make-up and wearing old clothes, like Marmar.

• **Skin problems** – it's just horrible trying to manage spots or acne when there are so many other things to deal with in adolescence. Your understanding and a listening ear will help. It is so hard, and spots don't clear up overnight. Buy your daughter the best skin creams and cleansers you can afford. Go for natural or organic products rather than those containing chemicals that can irritate the skin. Sodium laureth sulphate and preservative parabens are among the chemicals to be avoided.

- **Self-harming** - see V is for Violins, page 118.
- **Creepy crawlies** - girls with their long hair and tendency to cuddle up to each other create a fantastic breeding ground for nits (head lice)! I have spent hours combing for nits and a lot of money on products that promise to kill both nits and their eggs, but in the end found that you have to use lots of hair conditioner and comb out the hair several times a week in order to break the nit/egg cycle. Oddly, though, these nit/egg sessions have provided a chance to have a catch up chat or to watch *The Sound of Music* for the thirty-fourth time.

Threadworm is another hideous thing to deal with. What could be more distressing than discovering a worm is the cause for your bottom and vagina itching like mad in the middle of the night? Seek treatment from the chemist for these little blighters immediately.

What would Marmar do?

She was ahead of her time with healthy eating. We were given homemade yoghurt (yuck), homemade bread (when toasted it would break your teeth), and vitamin tablets every day. We were rarely ill. Marmar saw illness as some kind of failure, so she would drum into us that it was important to have something raw with every meal.

I think she's right about this. How about asking your daughter what raw vegetables and fruit she likes, hates or would be willing to try? If you can, try some unusual ones and have a blind tasting.

As a child, my younger sister hated frozen peas, which were the convenience vegetable of our childhood. Marmar's approach to this was to insist she ate the same number of peas as her age. I remember the peas on her plate increasing from seven to eight and so on. I must ask her if she now eats 48 peas.

What I liked about this was Marmar's creativity combined with her gentle insistence that 'no peas' was not an option and that trying a few was expected.

Vaginas

> *We have always been the kind of family to wander round in the nude, then one day my daughter locked the bathroom door – the 'don't come in' phase had arrived.*

Jim, dad of a daughter aged 11

Your daughter's vagina is at the heart of her puberty, her sex life and her journey into motherhood. No wonder that there are so many weird and wonderful names for this sacred part of your daughter's body. In Caitlin Moran's book, *How To Be A Woman* (Ebury Press 2012) she writes about the hundreds of tweets she received after asking people for their childhood name for the vagina. My favourite was 'Birmingham City Centre'. Pet names are fine, but it's important that by the time your daughter is school age she knows the word 'vagina' and what it is.

A daughter's body developing into a woman's will be a source of intrigue, excitement and possibly disgust to her. For you, maybe it's the same, but it can also feel sad, as it's hard evidence that she's growing up. Long before her breasts bud or pubic hair sprouts, you might spot your toddler fiddling with her 'front bottom'. She'll shriek on finding out that babies come out of the same hole they went in by, and that the same hole leaks blood once a month until she's nearly her grandma's age.

Puberty strikes a girl anytime from eight to 14, with 11 being the average age according to NHS guidelines. Your daughter may still be at primary school, but her hormones are hard at work giving her the appearance, moods and attitude of a teenager, which will be further stimulated by the media she watches.

" My challenge at the moment is dealing with my 12-year-old's attitudes which are taken from US TV shows and a tendency to act much more grown up than she actually is... "

Julie, mum to a daughter aged 12 and a son aged 15

Periods

" Women's complaints. "

Marmar's name for periods

As parents, we can help our daughters to cope with the changes of puberty by our attitude towards it. Periods were not discussed at all in my childhood home, even with three daughters growing up. I remember phoning Marmar at work to tell her my period had started and she said, 'Oh, you're a woman now, do you know what to do?' and that was it. Although most of my friends received a similar response from their mothers, I think it would have helped if Marmar had asked more about what I knew instead of assuming I had the right information, let alone how I felt about it!

Parents today report feeling embarrassed, awkward and even sad at the thought of talking to their daughters about periods. Buying her a good book or forwarding web links are helpful, but what do you think your daughter wants from you at this turning point in her life? I have noticed though, that some daughters are very straightforward about periods and will talk freely about being 'on' in front of parents and friends, including boys. On the other hand, some are embarrassed and unable to tell you. This reluctance can hurt your feelings especially if you feel you have done your best to let your daughter know she can talk to you about anything.

Talk to her; find out what she knows already. Be clear about who is providing her sanitary protection, and check that she has spares in her school bag and some pain relief medication if she suffers from bad period pains.

If she looks embarrassed you could say you feel that way too. Perhaps you won't be embarrassed, but however you feel, it's important to communicate to her that you're here to support her. Mums might want to share with their daughter what their first period was like and how they dealt with telling their parents. A first period is a symbol of transition from childhood to adulthood. We can choose to acknowledge the onset of puberty as something to celebrate.

" *We took each of our daughters out for a meal when they started their periods and gave them a piece of jewellery. They loved the attention, and we wanted to mark this special time in their and our lives.* "

Jenny, mum of three grown daughters

There are some extraordinary rituals and celebrations that take place in different cultures to mark the start of periods. The Urubu-Kaapor tribe of Brazil cut off a girl's hair and isolate her from the village for fasting and education. Once her hair has grown back to shoulder length, she is considered to be ready for marriage. Can you imagine your daughter going through that?

In our culture, your daughter is more likely to nip down to the shops with your wallet, buy some tampons and chocolate, be grumpy and ask you to write a note to excuse her from PE lessons.

" Periods are NOTHING to be embarrassed about. Conversations should sometimes take place around dads and brothers so that girls don't feel like boys can't or don't know about them, or that they happen! Too often girls feel ashamed of their bodies working exactly as Mother Nature wants them to. "

Flossie, aged 20

Periods checklist

- Mums, remember your first period and how was it for you? What was your parents' reaction? Could they have said or done something that was more useful? Tell your daughter about your experience and let her know there is no such thing as a stupid question. An older sister can be a great help to a younger sister in managing puberty.
- Celebrate her first period by taking her out for a special meal or buying her a gift to mark this passage into adulthood.
- Towels or tampons? Your daughter might prefer towels to start with. Keep them in the loo where it's easy for her to find them and for you to see when it's time to replenish. Don't feel you have to hide them from her brothers or her dad – it's a normal part of her life – and, of course, yours. Show her what to do if she stains her underwear or the sheets, especially if she's at someone else's house! Diary Doll period pants provide extra protection for girls with heavier periods, or mums with dodgy pelvic floors!

Let's talk about sex

" My daughter came home from school one day and announced, 'I now know where babies come from. They come from mummy's penis.' "

Phil, father of Edie who was seven at the time

As your daughter's sexuality develops, how do we communicate with her about sex, sexuality and staying safe? The alarming rise in the millions of children watching online porn means that our daughters' generation have had to cope with the expectation to look and act like a stick thin, pubic hair-free porn star.

" I admire my friend's mum. She talks openly about sex and what her daughter can and can't do when she is in a relationship. This is really important because girls often become 'blinded with love,' despite her boyfriend treating her badly. Knowing how and where to set the boundaries is key. "

Kara, aged 15

As well as contraception choices, you and your daughter need to know about sexually transmitted infections (STIs), or venereal diseases (VDs) as they were called in my day.

I can't recall sex education classes at school including information about making good relationships; they were just about the biology of sex. It is on offer now in the UK through the sex and relationships part of the curriculum (usually delivered in PSHE lessons), but as with technology safety, don't leave it to your daughter's school or to playground rumours, TV sitcoms or YouTube clips to educate your daughter on sexual health or the ingredients of a loving relationship.

> *" I know my parents worry about me staying out and the consequences of some actions, for example pregnancies and violent relationships. "*

Shania, aged 17

Our job is to help our daughter value herself and her body, so she doesn't lose her virginity, drunk in a park to the first bloke who pays her some attention.

Our job is to help her think carefully about peer pressure. Boys and girls may say they have lost their virginity or are 'shagging non-stop'. We can support her to wait until she feels ready for sex. We can tell her we believe that sex is not something to be taken lightly and that it is best between couples who have a love and respect for each other that has grown over time.

Our job is to appreciate that it can be hard to say 'no' or 'not yet' and to admire our daughter for any signs that she is resisting following the crowd.

Pregnancy
The day you find that your daughter is pregnant will be somewhere on a scale from wonderful at one end, disaster at the other. I remember talking to a lady who fell pregnant accidentally when she was just 17 and still at school. She was terrified of telling her mum,

convinced this would provoke anger, tears and an appointment at an abortion clinic. She finally plucked up the courage to say those two words, 'I'm pregnant.' To her astonishment, her mum looked at her, smiled and opened her arms up to give her a hug. Instead of being angry, her mum said she understood how hard that had been for her daughter to tell her this news.

What can parents do to help their daughter engage with puberty, and find the path to a happy and safe sex life?

" I hope our teens will remember that we were sensitive to their awkwardness and embarrassments, and that we were approachable on ANY subject. "

Carol Smillie, mum of two daughters and a son, TV presenter and co-founder of Diary Doll period pants

Checklist for parents on sex

* A daughter with high self-esteem and a positive relationship with her parents is more likely to wait to have sex within a loving relationship than to be promiscuous and do something she regrets.
* The earlier you talk about sex and relationships the easier it will be for you and your daughter to expand those conversations as she grows older and needs more information and advice. Find the books and websites that seem right to you. Ask your friends and family, GP, teachers or youth leaders what they recommend.
* Find out what she knows about contraception and STIs. Be prepared with relevant facts and information. The alternative is that she will learn about it from a YouTube clip or from her friends.

- Keep up to date with what is being taught (or not) at school on sex and relationships, but don't rely on the school to do the job for you.
- Dads, brothers, boyfriends and other key male role models have a vital part to play in forming her view of what a decent bloke is like. There is more about this in Secret 4 (see pages 164-184).
- If your daughter's boyfriend dumps her, listen, offer tea and sympathy but avoid saying, 'There are plenty more fish in the sea.'

" Girls experience every emotion throughout their teens and I think sometimes parents can understate or belittle that. It may not seem like 'true love', 'heartbreak', 'devastation' to an adult, but for the child/teen it is very real and raw. Support is needed more in these moments rather than disregard. "

Susie, aged 23

" My daughters were shrieking and squirming when I showed them how to put on a condom properly using a broom handle. But I didn't want to assume they would learn how to do this properly behind the bike sheds! "

Stuart, dad of three daughters who were six, ten and 12 at the time of the demonstration

Is she a lesbian or bisexual?

Although we're living in a time when it is easier to be openly gay than ever before, it still creates prejudice and potential difficulties for our daughters. Even the word 'gay' is liberally used as an insult. Parents might be fine with their daughter being gay, but other family members may have a different view and be judgmental. Whatever her sexual preference is, whether it is a phase or permanent, she will always need your unconditional love, acceptance and support so that she can grow up to be a fabulously confident woman and – as being gay definitely doesn't rule out having children – mother.

> 66 *I want to thank my mum and dad for loving me even when I have done something wrong.* 99
>
> Millie, aged 14

That is all the space I want to give to the V-signs. If you are struggling with any of these issues, you are not alone. Get help to take action for yourself and your daughter. There is help for you in the Directory, and please visit www.darlingdaughters.org for current information and support.

A parent's story

> 66 *My daughter Talia is 11 and my son Jack is 14. I work full time, and weekday mornings are really mad trying to get everyone out of the house on time. I have never been a breakfast eater, as I just can't face food at that time of the day. I'm not much of a cook and*

find the whole thing of family meals a bore really. The kids have always had cereal and juice before school, while I have my shower and do a million other things. However, when Talia started in year six, she came home saying she was 'fat' and was going on a diet. I was horrified, she's not fat at all, and I don't want her saying things like that. The next day she didn't eat breakfast, and this went on for over a week. She also started looking in the mirror all the time, and the 'fat' talk continued, not helped AT ALL by Jack who told her she looked like a whale in her school uniform. She was also glued to a programme about the dangers of obesity. I felt panicky and worried she would develop an eating disorder and mentioned it to a good friend at work. She gave me a number for a nutritionist and I went to see her by myself initially. She listened carefully, and she asked me about the family's meals and eating habits. It was only then I realised that if I didn't eat breakfast, why would my daughter think it was necessary? I started the next day with porridge and apple, and tried hard to be relaxed about it. The nutritionist also saw Talia and me together, and she helped us to understand what our body needs to grow properly, give us energy and keep us healthy. She also showed us height and weight charts so she could see she wasn't overweight. She talked about health, not fat. Two months on, and Talia is much better and we are both trying out new recipes and I talk less about my own appearance. I *have also discovered how much more energy I have to get through the day by starting it with breakfast!* 99

Janice, mum of an 11-year-old daughter
and a 14-year-old son

I have included Janice's story because it shows just how easy it is for us mums to be unaware of how much our own habits are picked up by our daughters. I like the way that Janice didn't panic in front of her daughter and wisely sought help to make changes as follows:

- She made the connection that Talia would be more likely to eat breakfast if she set a good example and ate it too.
- She felt out of her depth and panicky, but she found the right professional advice early on, before Talia's change in eating habits and negative body image thoughts developed further.
- She went alone first, to get advice, and then included her daughter so they could learn together about good nutrition focused on health, not weight.

I would add that she could also have had a quiet word with Jack about not commenting on his sister's appearance!

What would Marmar say about problems?

66 *Least said, soonest mended.* 99

Marmar

I'm not sure I agree with her on this one, but she was trying to say that sometimes there are no clear solutions and that you just have to move on. Parents with sons report that sometimes boys are more straightforward to deal with and that they move on more readily compared to daughters.

Girls can be tempted to over analyse things, and parents can also reach for the therapist's help before trying other home-grown solutions first.

I would love to meet a twenty-first-century daughter growing up completely unscathed by technology, friends, harmful substances or body and self-esteem issues. But I have witnessed plenty of daughters who are navigating their way through these V-signs and emerging into fabulous women, and it was their parents who made all the difference in their ability to do that with their honesty, their persistence and their love. I hope you have found something here and in the Directory that will help you. Please let me know at www.darlingdaughters.org.

> " *Yes, I've staggered home drunk, and not revised for an exam as much as I could have, but I always knew that I was letting myself down more than anyone else. Mum and Dad have brought me up to take responsibility for myself by not hovering over me all the time. That's been so valuable now I've gone to uni.* "
>
> Clare, aged 20

What are you taking away from the third secret? Make some notes on pages 281–284.

The V-signs:

Know what is essential to keep your
darling daughter safe and happy.

REMINDER

Take out of this secret what you feel is right for you and
your daughter.

SECRET 4: DADS

USE YOUR POWER WISELY

> ❝ *I hope that my daughters remember us with a smile and a warm glow in their hearts.* ❞
>
> Andy, dad of three daughters and a son

Discover the secrets of:
- Your role in your daughter's life.
- Dealing with balls-ups and breakthroughs.
- Acknowledging your power and how to use it wisely.
- Your most important building project.

In my dreams, every girl in the world would have a fantastic father. A dad who is kind and decent and would never hurt her.

A dad who loves his daughter without question.

A dad whose face lights up when she comes into the room.

A dad who thinks of his daughter at every stage of her life as a person with unlimited potential.

A dad who waits and watches patiently when his toddler or his teenage daughter rejects him.

A dad who, when his daughter thinks of a good man, she thinks of him.

I would have loved a dad like that. My dad struggled with depression for most of his adult life. He wrestled with a constant quest to find truth and meaning in life as a reaction to his own childhood growing up in a strict Christian home. I believe this got in the way of his ability to engage fully with fatherhood. He did what he could to bring up his three daughters with the knowledge he had at the time.

I will always be grateful to him for his enjoyment of having daughters and not wishing they were sons.

My dad was born in 1930 in New Zealand – as was my mum – and was the first person in his family to go to university, which led to a life-long career as an academic, teaching philosophy. He met Marmar during a tomato fight in the university library, falling for her big brown eyes and mischievous sense of humour. They sailed to England, married and set up home in London where they remained for the rest of their lives.

Part of my dad's unhappiness came from years of wishing he could move back to New Zealand or Australia, but Marmar wouldn't budge. She was determined to bring up her daughters in England and give them a British education. My dad had a rather old-fashioned view. He questioned the value of educating girls and this caused a number of rows between my mum and dad and had a limiting effect on my own educational aspirations.

In his later years something special happened to him. He became a grandfather, and like so many dads, he embraced being a grandfather with a delight that was a joy to observe. He was interested in his grandchildren and they, naturally, enjoyed his company in the way that children gravitate towards adults that they feel comfortable around.

> 66 *I loved the way he laughed and smiled and sang songs with me. He's in Heaven having a big rest.* 99
>
> My then four-year-old daughter remembering her granddad at his funeral

Like my dad, my husband has also found it tough at times to understand the role of a father in bringing up daughters. Many dads I have talked to scratch their heads and wonder if they're just needed to be a walking wallet, chauffeur and spider catcher. They want to be more involved with their kids than their own dads were, but they are not sure where to start. Sometimes dads say they find it easier with their sons, but they find their daughters a mystery. If you feel that way, you're not alone. I hope this fourth secret will help you to feel more confident and less mystified about being a father to your darling daughter.

Your starting point, like mine, on raising a daughter is coloured by your own dad, especially if you had a sister as you will have memories of how he behaved towards her.

How do you learn how to be a dad? You are born with the skills you need. You think about your own dad, or others you know and what they're like. You copy the parenting that worked for you. You try not to repeat the parenting you hated. You vow you'll never repeat some of the sayings you heard from your parents:

> " *Something my parents used to say to me that I promised myself I'd never say when I became a dad, but now say all the time: 'Well it wouldn't have happened if you'd been wearing your slippers'.* "

Jesse Quinn, father of a young daughter and
a son, and bass player in the band Keane

What is the role of a dad in his daughter's life?

You might be confused about your role as your daughter's dad. You might feel you're like a spare part because what you offer is thrown back at you, but if you don't read anything else, read this:

TIPS

As your daughter's dad:
You are important.
What you say is important.
What you think and what you feel is important.
What you do is important.

Your number one priority is to take your job of fatherhood seriously as your daughter needs you throughout her life. Why?

- You have a unique and powerful role to help your daughter feel lovable and capable.
- From you, she will learn what males are like, especially if you're the only man in the family.
- You have the power to help her feel good about herself, so she does not rush off with the first bloke who pays her some attention.

You can choose to see these three tasks as opportunities to be closely involved in the upbringing and well-being of your daughter, but it will be challenging at times. Remember, nobody says on their deathbed that they wished they had spent more time at work.

66 Keep being interested in what they do and find interesting, and encourage them and support them as well as you possibly can in those things. 99

Tom, dad of three daughters aged 13, 17 and 20

Balls-ups and breakthroughs

66 War is easier than daughters. 99

From George R. R. Martin's *Game of Thrones*, and said by the character Eddard 'Ned' Stark

Parenting is a life's work in progress. A mum aged 95 recently endured her 56-year-old son having surgery for cancer and out of worry rang her daughter-in-law 12 times on the day of his operation.

It usually gets easier as you and your daughter clock up the years together, but until you take your last breath, you are her dad.

In all those years of being around your kids, expect mistakes or balls-ups to happen.

At my Darling Daughters live events, I ask the dads to gather away from the women in the room to talk about where they have made some spectacular balls-ups with their daughters. They're a bit nervous to start with, but after cracking a joke or two, they come up with story after story. Such as the times they tried to teach their daughter how to ride a bike and she stormed off, forgot to pick their daughters up from school or when homework help became a homework fight.

Having a chance to chat with other dads about balls-ups is reassuring – you're not the only one that finds parenting daughters baffling. At these sessions, sometimes a dad will confess he's stuck for ideas and the others will chip in with what they have discovered 'works' with their daughters. That kind of dad-to-dad support is gold. Especially these days when dads feel isolated. They lack extended family support, and are up against it trying to hold down a career and be a caring partner let alone finding some 'me' time. And there is the nagging guilt of trying to match up to the Father's Day card proclaiming you to be 'The Best Dad in the World'.

> 66 *You can't be a perfect dad, but take breaks from busyness and spend at least some periods of quality time with your daughter.* 99
>
> Pete, dad to a daughter aged 14

Do you feel the pressure to be Superman and super dad? When that pressure rules, it creates a breeding ground for guilt and crumbling confidence. Guilt drags you down. I sometimes see inappropriate or over-the-top actions spring from guilt. For example, the dad who feels guilty that he doesn't see much of his daughter, so he gives her presents or cash. Guilt and pressure send stress levels rocketing, which magnifies the problems. Balls-ups can feel like catastrophes. A battle to get your daughter to put on her coat can ruin an outing to the park, and end up with you shouting and saying or doing things you regret. Frustration and guilt then take charge. With these kinds of incidents it's a case of calming down as best you can - step outside for a few minutes for example. Sit down and tell her you love her and apologise for your behaviour, without adding 'but if' justifications about her behaviour. The next time a park trip is coming up, you can ask her what's needed before you can go to the park.

Guilt – tell it where to go

> **"** I felt guilty of wanting to smack them or shut them up as if they were buzzing mosquitos when they were just being kids, mucking about. It was my stuff; I was tired and grumpy. **"**

Alan, dad of three daughters

If you want to lessen the power of guilt, it starts with recognising where your guilt comes from.

Make some notes in the back of the book about what or who causes you to feel guilty as a dad. Then, make some notes about what you would do if you replaced guilt with more positive thoughts, ideas and actions.

Breakthroughs

> **"** I used to motivate my daughters by offering to dance. Now I motivate them by threatening to dance! **"**

Jason, dad of teenage daughters

Among many things, I am thankful to dads for their ability to fix things. I'm not talking about a dripping tap, but about persevering to find solutions to problems. So, when it comes to solving a problem that is causing fights and arguments with your daughter – teaching her to ride a bike, letting you wash her hair or whose party she's going to, for example – what are your options? What have you tried so far? What do you see other dads doing that you could try?

" *As a parent there is a constant nagging worry that you are somehow getting things wrong. I think you just have to accept that you are, but that you are also getting some things right. You just have to hope that the balance goes in your favour in the end.* "

Hugh Dennis, dad of a daughter and a son, and actor and comedian, who played Dad in the family sitcom *Outnumbered*

I don't know what your wider experience of females is, but if it would help, here are some clues about getting some breakthroughs with your daughter:
1. Your daughter is emotionally driven.
2. When your daughter is having a tantrum or she's upset or sad, the first thing you should do is sit with her and listen.
3. You don't have to DO anything or fix anything.
4. If you feel yourself getting worked up, sit down, keep your arms unfolded and relax your shoulders.
5. Girls work out what they feel or what they want to do by talking about it, which can take a while. You can try asking her to tell you 'What's the most important thing?' or 'What's the most difficult part of this?'
6. Next, have a guess what she is feeling.

Just a few words will do: 'I can see you're cross that I said no.'
You can also try to guess what she wants: 'I guess you wish I was the kind of dad who would say "yes" to giving you what you want?'

" My dad is terrible at answering questions. He'll either ignore you or spend hours replying without actually answering the question. "

Talia, aged 18

A dad's story

> **❝** I work a lot of night shifts, so when I can, I pick up my eight-year-old daughter, Rebecca, from school. Sometimes, I might not have seen her for a few days due to work shifts, so I can't wait to see her. What hurts is that she doesn't look that pleased to see me, or want to talk to me or tell me about her day. I offer to take her to the park on the way home or for an ice cream, but she just shrugs her shoulders and mumbles at me. I then get annoyed and tell her to speak properly, she is then in a mood with me, so we just go home. I was getting fed up with this so I asked my wife where I was going wrong, and she said try and think of it from Rebecca's point of view. She's had a long day at school and she might not be in the mood to talk, and my work shift complications are of no interest to an eight-year-old. My wife said Rebecca is often the same with her, so she handles it by not saying too much, or she'll try something like, 'What was the one thing that you heard about today that you haven't heard before?' It doesn't have to be a school thing, it could be anything, but it's an easier question to answer than 'How was your day?' My wife always takes a snack along at pick up time as she said we have no idea how much Rebecca has eaten during the day, and her blood sugar needs a boost by then. So this week, I have picked up our daughter from school, given her a hug and then a snack. I stopped asking loads of questions, and let silence

take over. It's been alright actually, more relaxed, and she's looked happier to see me when I pick her up. **"**

Jonny, dad of an eight-year-old daughter

I have included Jonny's story because it's a good example from a busy dad who is trying to be loving and involved with his daughter, but who admits he finds it hard when his efforts are rejected. However, he doesn't sulk and blame his daughter, but seeks to understand her better.

- He asks his wife for ideas and listens to what she has to say, and then acts on it.
- He realises the importance of his daughter's feelings, instead of focusing on his own feelings of rejection and disappointment.
- He has sorted out snacks to boost his daughter's blood sugar.
- He has shown her affection by giving her a hug and he has seen the value in staying silent or asking different questions.

Act your age not hers

What kind of adult do you want to be when your daughter is being difficult? If she is being sullen, stubborn, grumpy or obstinate or is shouting or swearing at you, how do you respond?

Shout back?

Storm off?

Sulk?

Threaten her? 'If you don't stop that right now I will…'

Insist you're right?

Any of these tactics might gain you some power in the short term and fix the problem, but how about the long term? Maybe you're OK with using these methods to sort out your daughter.

The truth is you may feel powerless at times, but just by **being** her dad, you have huge amounts of power.

You've got the power: use it wisely.

Physical power

To your daughter, your size, your voice and your strength can be as terrifying as confronting a lion. Your physical power can be intimidating to her, but it will help her if you bring yourself closer to her size by sitting or squatting next to her. Keep your arms down and relaxed, instead of folded or with hands on hips. Use eye contact, but in her teen years she may want you to avert your gaze. Try to reduce the volume of your voice. She needs to **feel safe** with you, If she is taller than you, you still have significant power and influence because you are her dad.

Mental and emotional power

It's useful at this point to recall Secret 1 – understanding how your daughter grows up – and Secret 2 – modelling your values and living by them. These chapters emphasised that your opinions and values and the way these are expressed will affect your daughter's view of herself, her self-esteem and the life choices she makes.

> " *No matter the amount of effort or success we achieve, our father will forever see us as a disappointment and is vocal about this.* "
>
> Anna, aged 18

If you want to grow a positive sustainable relationship with your daughter, these tips may help:

- **Father of the bride. Work out your principles, rather than detailed rules** for yourself as her dad. If you're wondering how to get to the heart of how to describe what you want to be to your daughter, imagine it's her wedding day and you're making the 'father of the bride' speech. What will you want to say about her and your hopes for her going forwards into her new married life?

- **Match your parenting to your values**. Redirect your energies on what really matters to you without 'shoulding'.
- **Respect has to be earned by both of you**. If you want your daughter to respect you, you need to show respect to her.
- **Trust your parental instinct**. If you have a hunch that something isn't right, investigate it.
- **Look after your relationship with her mum** as best you can. Criticising her mum will harm your daughter.
- **Forgive yourself, forgive her**. Mistakes are normal and can be useful learning. Let go of grudges and see forgiveness as a strength.

My favourite painting is *The Prodigal Daughter* by the artist Charlie Mackesy. As in Jesus' parable of the prodigal son, which is related in St Luke's Gospel (15:11-32), the daughter featured in Mackesy's work ran away and is returning home poor and desperate. What I love about this painting is the values that the father is showing his daughter. He is forgiving her, he is embracing her, and he has used his strength to lift her up, even though she is fully grown. I keep this painting very visible in our home as a prompt for the values that my husband and I try to live by as parents to our daughters.

Using symbols, such as a painting, a photo, a piece of music, words or a lock of your daughter's hair in your wallet, can help to remind you of your love for your unique daughter, and the values that you want to demonstrate to her.

What would help you live out your values? You might want to write a list of ideas in the notes pages at the back of the book.

" I hope she appreciates my jokes in time, my interest in her, the effort I put into preparing home cooked food, and I really hope she remembers that I loved her deeply even though I couldn't say it very often. "

Pete, dad of a daughter aged 14

Your most important building project

If I were about to have a baby, I would give my husband the excellent book *Commando Dad*, written by Neil Sinclair, an ex-Royal Engineers commando turned dad and childminder. Neil wanted some clear instructions, as he would have found in a Royal Engineers' manual, about what to do as a dad. He couldn't find what he was looking for anywhere, so he wrote the book. Like Neil, I am hoping to offer you some straightforward, helpful guidelines.

I appreciate you are busy and want answers. You might be the kind of dad who has a handle on ideas for raising daughters. Forgive me if you have heard any of this before, but these ideas have worked for many dads I have encountered. Sometimes, you hear about a parenting tip, but if it doesn't meet a need for you at the time, you'll probably bin it. However, as your daughters grow up, we, and they change, and so it can be worth considering ideas you may have heard elsewhere. I also find as I get older that I simply can't remember everything I know, but the more I practise it, the more likely it is to become automatic.

The three essential tasks as dad of a daughter are:

1. Build her mind so she is curious
Help your daughter build a great mind of her own by asking for her opinion before giving yours. Share with her what makes you curious, and compliment her when she shows curiosity or takes

a risk. Her questioning or arguing may drive you mad, but you can tell her that she has argued her case well, even if your answer still needs to be 'no'.

You have a great opportunity to teach her – not just stereotypical dad jobs like how to mend a puncture or wire a plug – but about your passions too. Modern families don't trap men and women into traditional roles, but what your daughter will notice is your passion for something, whether it's cooking, politics or DIY. Likewise, avoid steering her into stereotypical female pursuits. She will learn from you best if you calmly and patiently follow the I, We, You formula for teaching:

I take out the bins.

We both take out the bins.

You take out the bins.

2. Build her heart so she feels valued

What to do:

- Look up, smile and say 'hello' when you see her.
- Be affectionate – hugs, kisses, cuddles and a pat on the back help, even if she tells you that your whiskers prickle, or worse.
- Be interested in her - ask her what she liked about her day. Ask her what she heard today that she had never heard before.
- Communicate with notes, texts, photos or emails saying you're thinking about her, that you love her, that you hope her day is going well, or share a joke that you think she would like.
- Write her a letter at least once a year describing what you admire and love about her.
- If you're too busy to show an interest, she won't care what's making you busy. She'll just conclude she is boring and that it's not worth initiating the effort of engaging with you.
- Offer your time on her terms even if that means doing something that you don't like.

- **Share an adventure** – take her away for a few days camping, walking or cycling.
- Have a **date** with her, and if you're sitting in a cafe with her, **switch off your phone** so she knows that you're paying her attention.

> 66 *A dad I know organised a weekend cycling trip for dads and daughters. We stayed in a youth hostel and all mucked in with cooking and planning the cycling. I had no idea how something like that would really help me get to know my daughter. I know what to do with my sons, but finding a way to engage with her had been problematic before that cycling weekend.* 99

Tony, dad of two sons and a daughter

What to say:
- Frequently tell her **what you love and admire about her**. It could be something as simple as praising her willingness to help her brother with his Lego bricks. **Specific praise** from you builds her up from the inside and keeps her going all day, like a good breakfast. Praise her by saying 'I love watching you... (swim, dance, play, etc.).'
- If she has a problem, have a **guess at what she is feeling** without feeling that you need to fix the problem. For example, 'I guess you're upset because you left your phone at Ellie's.'
- **Girls can't stand criticism** from anyone, especially their dads. If you want to challenge her behaviour, she is more likely to listen to you if you listen to her to without interruption or jumping in with criticism or sarcasm.

> *" My dad put me to bed every night to say prayers, talk and tell me stories. Being a good listener is one of the best things you can be especially if you do not agree or like what I am saying. "*

Chloe, now aged 21

3. Build her vision of a good man

My friend was in the car recently singing along to a song that Robbie Williams wrote for his daughter. There is a line in it about Robbie advising his daughter to make sure that whoever she gives her heart to that he is worth it, and if not to keep searching!

Studies show that girls who have a close relationship with their dad are far less likely to choose unsuitable partners and more likely to achieve higher grades at school.

If you want your daughter to **choose a decent man** and not run off with the first boy who pays her some attention, then you have a great opportunity to show what a decent man is like.

Look again at your parenting values and weld them to your parenting. Watch films and TV programmes, including soaps (if that's what your daughter's into), and talk about the male characters and what they're like. **Talk about the men you admire and why**.

> *" I admire Sir Paul McCartney. He created a real world environment that ensured his children could grow up with strong values and an understanding of those around us, no matter what 'class' they were in. "*

Michael, dad of two grown-up daughters

Tell her the stories and show her pictures of the **men in your family** of previous generations and how they influenced you. When boyfriends show up, welcome them. Can you remember what you felt like when you went to your girlfriend's home and met her parents? I hope they were more welcoming than this dad:

> *I took my boyfriend home for the first time, and when Dad came in, I said, 'Dad, this is Sam.' Dad looked at him and said, 'Hello Sam, now get out.' After that, I didn't bother to take boyfriends home for years!*

Mary, mum of three grown-up children

Talk about the women you admire for their minds and their actions, not their looks or their bodies. Talk about what you admire in her mum and other women in the family.

What do the other women in your life know?

What do you think your partner would make of these father/daughter relationship-building tasks? You could (if you don't already know) ask your partner what her dad did, or didn't do, to help her build her mind, heart and expectation of a good man. You could also ask your own sisters, other female relatives and friends for their experiences of your father. Ask them to help you understand your daughter and what kind of dad she needs.

Raising a daughter in a partnership

In the madness of modern family life, it's easy to fall into the trap of letting your relationship with your partner become a habit that is at best reliable, but could also be stale and stressful. Unkindness and resentment can build up into a competition of who is the most tired, stressed or taken for granted.

You may have heard that raising children glues couples together for life, but it can also rip the life (and sometimes the sex) out of your relationship. I am no relationship expert, but I am trained to understand the effects of poor parental relationships on bringing up children. Keeping your relationship healthy (even if you are no longer together) is vital if you both want to parent well and be consistent. If you are a couple, perhaps the best investment of your time will be regular dates with your partner. On these dates, limit talk about the children to the first half an hour or the first course of the meal.

So, three things to build in your daughter and a relationship to treasure, but as well as that, just…

… be a boy!

During my childhood, growing up with my sisters and going to a girls' school, my dad was the only male with whom I spent any time. Before boyfriends appear, girls learn the most about the male of the species from their dad and their brothers, so seize the chance to show your daughter what boys can be like and how they can think about women. You may have to let her know that if she chooses skimpy revealing clothes, boys will be more interested in her looks than in her wonderful mind. Help her to learn how men 'tick', what they're interested in and what shuts them down.

Dads are often natural instigators of fun, jokes, and games and, as Marmar said, 'larking about'. Teasing can be light-hearted fun, but it can go too far, especially for sensitive daughters. Family life can be too serious and stressful, so be a clown, but also encourage your partner and children to be playful too.

66 Well, of course, I WANT to be remembered as a dynamic, funny, interesting and handsome superhero (perhaps without the pants-over-trousers thing). Doesn't everyone? 99

Dad of two daughters aged 13 and 16

What would Marmar do?

 I have a favourite photo of my parents sitting at the table in their Christmas cracker hats. They were well into their retirement by then, but still able to be a priceless support team to my family. My husband and I both worked, and my parents provided some childcare and also the occasional childfree weekend away that definitely helped us strengthen our marriage.

Marmar was also very busy volunteering and flitting around friends and family. Dad's knees had packed up after years of squash playing that meant he was often stuck at home. Many times, Marmar would be heading out for the day and leave him with a job or two, saying: 'You've got nothing to do, and all day to do it in.'

I'm telling you this because once your daughters have grown up and gone, keeping up or finding new hobbies is vital for your twilight years once you finally stop work. My dad left it too late to sort out his knees, and in doing so put an end to his cycling and walking, which he loved to do. But way before your retirement, your darling daughter will be fascinated by what you love to do. Seeing her dad engrossed in something helps her learn the value of hobbies and interests, even if she doesn't share similar interests.

Me time for dads

Some dads feel guilty about having time away from their family. If they work long hours with a big commute, they can feel it's unfair to want more time in which to do their own thing. Guilt is an energy drain, so I want you to consider instead the value to you, your partner and your daughter if you take some 'me time'.

If it's been a while since you gave any time to a hobby, let me ask you these questions:

What did you love to do before kids came along?

What was it about that interest or hobby that you enjoyed?

What could you do to bring it back into your life now, even in a reduced version?

You'll find these questions repeated on the notes pages (see page 284) so that you can record your answers.

Having interests outside work and family fuels your ability to be a fantastic dad to your daughter. You're not being selfish so long as you also help your partner have 'me time'.

You are important. What you say, what you do and what you feel are powerful in your darling daughter's life. Thank you for all that you do contribute to her development into being a great girl, a wonderful woman, and for using your power wisely.

What are you taking away from the fourth secret? Jot down your thoughts and ideas on the notes pages.

Dads:

Use Your Power Wisely.

REMINDER

Take out of this secret what you feel is right for you and your daughter.

SECRET 5: MUMS

DITCH THE GUILT – BE THE ROLE MODEL YOU WANT YOUR DAUGHTER TO HAVE

Discover the secrets of:
- Mums as role models and what does that mean?
- Guilt, finding your G-spot and getting rid of it.
- Career girls, and what is our message to our daughters about being a working mum?
- Why you are worth it and why 'me time' matters.

" *Massive thanks to my mum for basically raising my sister and me on her own, and for helping shape us to be the (pretty decent) people we are today.* "

Lula, aged 19

Hey mums, you are the biggest influence on how your darling daughter will turn out!

No pressure, then. I have been a parent for nearly a quarter of a century, and during those years of raising our three daughters, there have been times when the responsibility of being their role model has made me want to hide under the duvet for the day. Parenting already means nurturing and guiding our children. For many mums, you can add your work, running a home and fulfilling your partner's needs and wants to the list along with supporting elderly parents, other relatives and friends and caring for the family pet. Doing all of that and knowing that your daughter is watching, listening and taking mental notes of how you're measuring up as a woman and a mum is enough to make you reach for the gin. But being real about our fears and failings can be just what our daughters need too.

> " *Open up about yourself, and then your daughter will open up in return because we realise that when it comes down to it, we're all women and go through the same experiences in life and mums can give advice that our peers wouldn't have thought of.* "
>
> Lottie, aged 19

Our daughters use our life as a benchmark, so they can work out what kind of woman and mother they want to be. Many daughters have said to me that their mum is their greatest role model, but for some the opposite is true and they would not want to repeat how their mother raised them.

> " *I admire my mother and grandmother – they've both fostered loving, close, open and honest relationships with their daughters... and we've all turned out OK!* "

Marian, mum of twin daughters aged three and a baby son

As your daughter grows older, you might find yourself living with a younger version of yourself. My youngest daughter has my hands and legs; two of them have my voice. Long after I have gone, apart from physical similarities, they will still carry around with them what I said, what I did and what I valued. Sometimes, when we see the behaviour traits of which we're not so proud reappearing in our daughter, we react strongly. We don't want her to carry the same burdens.

> " *I know I have a problem with packing too much into the diary, and when I see my daughter doing the same thing, I tell her she's doing far too much.* "

Jan, mum of three teenage daughters

The pressure to be a good role model to our daughters can turn in to a toxic sewage of guilt and stress that drowns out the potential we have to be great role models. The message of this fifth secret is about telling guilt where to go. It also asks you to refocus and be the role model you want to be instead of the one you think you should be.

I must stress that there have been plenty of times when I have *not* felt like Eeyore nor wanted to hide under the duvet. There have also been times when I feel more hopeful about being a role model, enjoy it even, and in those moments, I can bounce out of bed like Tigger.

What kind of mum are you?

Every mum is unique, but there are some styles of mothering that can undermine our confidence. Forgive the labels, but I find that 'moaning mums' and 'perfect mums' are the types that have the potential to bring us all to our knees.

Moaning Milly

Why are mums more comfortable talking about their bad points than their good ones? A mum I worked with recently (I'll call her Ali for now) told me how the chat among the mums at school was becoming more of a competition of who was the most rubbish mum, like a kind of bad mum bake-off.

Each day at the school gate, the mums' chat was dominated by who had the worst kids, the grumpiest partner, the most demanding boss or the most disorganised house. No one was speaking up for the kids or themselves. Ali decided she had had enough of this competitive moaning and the colluding about what rubbish mums they were and the rubbish lives they lead.

She decided to only say something positive about her child, herself, her partner, her boss and her house. It was odd to begin with, and she was unsure about 'blowing her own trumpet', but it felt light and refreshing too. Some mums followed her example, but the significant change for Ali was she felt she had taken control of how that negativity at the school gate was affecting her.

I would love to see more mums give up the moaning and the self-deprecation. If you have moaning mums in your circles, don't let them dominate.

Mums are so important to the welfare of their family - we glue it together. On a bigger scale, strong families build strong societies.

Mums need to be cheered on and supported to do this vital role, not discounted or undervalued. And not just cheered on by Tesco's 'Mum of the Year' competition, but by everybody – politicians take note. End of rant.

Penelope Perfect
The other type of mum who is setting the bar far too high for the rest of us is Penelope Perfect. You might know a Penelope. She is the mum with the fabulous job who is hyper-organised, gorgeous and virtuous. Her children are popular and talented. She has them timetabled into all the right extracurricular activities where they are excelling at violin, dance and netball. Your heart sinks if your daughter says to you she wishes you were more like Penelope.

> " *I know a woman who has huge amounts of fun with her kids, paints the tennis shoes… but when she needs to discipline she's really firm, but fair.* "
>
> Janey Lee Grace, mum of a daughter and three sons, and radio presenter and author of *Imperfectly Natural Woman* (Crown House Publishing, 2005)

Penelope Perfects are often very good actresses, and sometimes once you get to know them you realise they are flawed like the rest of us. Sometimes, working as a 'Parenting Professional' has meant I can be perceived as a 'Penelope Perfect'. Nothing is further from the truth! I have noticed through my work that one of the best ways to reassure parents is to be honest about my parenting flaws without becoming a Moaning Milly!

I hope I can encourage you to make a fresh start and banish the power of any mum who is an unhelpful role model, one that zaps your energy and distracts you from being the role model you want *your* daughter to have.

Gather the mums you know who inspire you. Nick their ideas without a hint of guilt attached. There will be more about this in Secret 6 (see pages 206-229).

> " *I really admire my mum. I'm the youngest girl of five boys. We always had dinner around the table, we always had home-cooked food. Mum wore minimal make-up and was always glowing, she was daft as a brush and made me laugh every day. She laughed so hard she would sometimes wet herself. She loved dancing and having a few drinks, she sometimes smoked but swore blind she didn't. She was strict and terrified me sometimes, people loved her and she loved me more than anything.* "
>
> Jenny, mum of a baby daughter

In Secret 2, I asked you to think about what you might want to do if this was your last day as a parent. What would you want to do if this was the last day you could be a role model to your daughter? What would you *not* do?

On your notes pages, write a letter to your daughter sharing everything that you want your daughter to learn from you.

To my darling daughter,

....

....

....

All my love,

Mum xxxx

Recently, I asked a mum I was coaching what she would do if this were her last day with her daughter. She said within a heartbeat that she would go out with her daughter and take photos of her. She wouldn't bow to the pressure to join in play dates or cook the perfect dinner. She would be the mum she wanted to be, not the mum she thought she should be.

More good tips for mums

> 66 *Be kind but firm. Have a tender conversation just you and her once a week. Tell her your secrets of when you were her age. If you upset her, even if she's in the wrong, buy her a chocolate and apologise for being so firm. Get her to explain why she thinks she's in the right.* 99

Lottie, aged ten

Your daughter needs a mum, not a friend.

" Stop reading up on parenting advice and speak to your family! "

Rebecca, aged 14

- **Listen in silence** without interrupting, commenting, justifying or lecturing to help her open up and so develop a closer relationship.
- **Encourage and believe in her** to boost her self-esteem, especially when she doubts herself.
- **Apologise and forgive** yourself if you have done or said something you instinctively know is wrong. This will model the value of apologising and putting things right.
- **Stop saying you're hopeless**, disorganised, fat, cutting out carbs or worried about grey hairs. Daughters are telling us they do not find this helpful!
- **Model values** like those for dads from page 164. Without 'shoulding', be the mum you want her to learn from. Let her see your values in action.
- **Don't stop the mummy traditions.** You know those things like pet names, sitting on her bed chatting, leaving notes and the birthday and celebration rituals? Keep them going. Mums are brilliant at them.
- **Relax** and let her see you being less than perfect, having fun and sometimes throwing caution to the wind. It will help her to see that it's OK not to be perfect.
- **Look after yourself.** As they say on aeroplane safety warnings, please fit your own oxygen mask before fitting your children's. 'Me time' is a must, including for full-time mums.

- **Promote mums** and talk positively about what mothers have to contribute instead of being critical of how other mums are bringing up their children, what their partners and house are like or if they are stay-at-home or working mums.
- **Promote women** by talking about the importance of good female role models in the family, in society and in history. For inspiration on this topic, go to the Book and Movie Club on page 265 or to www.darlingdaughters.org.

> " Take some 'me time' even if you actually don't want to when they're little. You'll probably want to spend as much time with them as possible when they're young, but later on you'll need more of your own time and it will be much easier to get it if you don't feel (or aren't made to feel) guilty about it. "

Carrie, mum of two daughters aged 7 and 9

Me time

I can almost hear the groaning as I type that. Mums are notorious for putting themselves last and saying there simply isn't enough time for them to treat themselves or find five minutes' peace. When my daughters were little, going to the loo was sometimes the only chance of 'me time', and even that wasn't guaranteed!

I would say though that this is about choice. You can choose what you prioritise. If you find yourself saying (or thinking), 'I have no choice', try questioning that. Consider what it is costing you to have no time for yourself. Consider what 'me time' would give you instead. What would your idea of 'me time' be? Pampering and spa days are fabulous, but for many they are out of reach or perhaps not your idea of 'me time'.

What *would* give you a boost, that's within your control? Even if you just find five minutes to lie down and close your eyes and breathe deeply. Identify five things in each of these time slots and record them in your notes.

If I had five minutes for myself I would…

If I had a few hours for myself I would…

If I had a day or more for myself I would…

> " *I hope my daughter remembers I had a life of my own as well as being a mother, that I listened, that I had to work to achieve, that I tried to change things that I did not like and that I had good friendships.* "
>
> Clare, mum of a daughter aged 13 and a son aged 11

Career girls

From baby darlings onwards, we do our best to give our girls an education and opportunities that will build her towards joining the working world. During her school and college years, the careers advice on offer may be brilliant, but even if it's pathetic, I'm sure it will be much more adventurous than what was dished out to girls from previous generations. Our daughters have the largest choice of work opportunities - more so than at any other time in history - spread out before them like a banquet. It's never been a more exciting time to be a working girl, but too much choice can also leave you feeling unsure about what to choose.

Mums often ask me how to encourage daughters to find a career they love and one that fits in with motherhood. I need to be honest. I have rarely met a mum who has a full-time job and a family as well as other responsibilities, such as elderly parents, who is contentedly managing her load.

More often, sadly, she is stressed, exhausted and swamped with guilt. Her life feels like a house of cards that will collapse if one more card is added. I have asked mums in this position whether they would want their daughter to have their life when she is their age, and they answer 'No.' Sometimes realising this spurs them into action to make some changes to reduce the pressure.

At the same time, so many mums have no choice and have to manage the challenge working as a lone parent or as the bread-winning partner. I wish there was a clear answer to this complicated problem of how to combine work and motherhood, but I have yet to find one.

What I do see is the stress on mums that are shackled to high-flying jobs that may yield a high standard of living, but are not a recipe for happiness in families. The most contented mums I know are the ones with interesting part-time work.

> " *Live in the moment as much as you can and don't let distractions rob you of time with your daughter. I'm a mum working full-time outside of the home and sometimes I feel the need to be getting things done, but these times of play and being together are precious and I feel it's important to make time for them.* "

Rachel, mum of a two-year-old and working full-time

I have witnessed the sacrifices made in some families to launch their daughter's career. It creates huge pressure on many parents to earn enough money to pay for private schools and colleges. The numbers of women choosing NOT to have children because they can't see a way to fit them in or finance them is rising in the developed world.

Of course, your daughter may not become a mum, which would free her to focus on her career. What would you be doing now if you didn't have children?

My dad, like many of his generation, assumed he would provide for his daughters until we married and then our husbands would provide for us. I wouldn't dare or want to assume this for my own daughters.

They have grown up with me being a working mum. They expect and want to work if they become mothers. In our family, we are doing what we can to ensure our daughters find a career they love and at the same time can provide for themselves in the future. We value education, we value a hard working ethic and we encourage them to be adventurous before responsibilities take over. Should any of them choose full-time motherhood we would certainly value that too.

Before your daughter is in her mid-teens it will be time to have another values conversation with your partner. Coming up are some useful questions to discuss and answer together, about which you may want to make notes on page 288.

What are our hopes, fears and expectations about our daughter's career?

What are we prepared to offer (for example money, transport or work experience) to support our daughter in her career search?

What do we do if she chooses a career path that worries us?

> 66 *My husband has a fundamental problem with our daughter wanting to be an actress, but he's willing to let her give it a go providing she has another way of earning a living.* 99
>
> Laura, mum of three teenage daughters

So what is the message we want to give our darlings about their career? It will help your daughter if you keep up with developments in the job world. It has never been a more exciting time for girls going into work whatever their passions are, but at the same time, for some, the pressure is on to compete in a global market for the best jobs. Aside from earning money, consider the benefits working brings, whether your daughter has kids or not. The fast rise in 'mumpreneurs' (mums creating their own business, often working from home) has given thousands of mums the chance to build up a business with more flexibility.

What do we say to our daughters about combining work and family?

Mums I have asked about this say working gives them a life outside of the family, it sparks up their conversation, it helps them appreciate family time and it gives them some financial independence. It shows their daughters and their sons that today's mothers want to combine work and family, and that it can be done well.

> " *It took me a while to realise that I am happier and my relationship works better if I am working as well as my husband, and we are sharing the burden of work at home. Happy parents = happy daughters.* "
> Sasha, mum of two daughters aged two and five

Work/life balance may be the common phrase, but I would hope my daughters could aim for more than balance; I would want them to aim for the best of both worlds.

I say this to my daughters:

- Keep up a range of interests that build skills such as resilience, teamwork, leadership and problem solving. Finding a great career in a global market means employers will be interested in what else you can offer, not just academic results. They might also look at an applicant's social media profiles, so be careful what you put online.
- Aim for a working life, job or career that you are passionate about. Be adventurous especially before your options reduce, which they will when the time comes to consider the needs of a partner or children, or even your old mum and dad!
- Once you have children, you have the rest of your life to work. Your years spent raising children are irreplaceable. A wise lady with grown-up children said that to me when I was feeling very conflicted about trying to find a child-friendly job. I will always be grateful that her words delayed my decision to return to work after my second daughter was born.
- To leave your family and go out to work it needs to be worth it, and not just financially. Find the best childcare you can so that when you are at work, you feel free to work.
- Work at work; be at home at home. If you work from home, create clear boundaries – as if you were working outside the home – for when you're working. I have work clothes to wear at home, tempting though it is to stay in my pyjamas.
- Full-time mothers sometimes undervalue themselves; not helped by society's attitude, employers, family and friends. 'I'm just a mum' is a phrase I would love to ban. If you want to be a full-time mum and it works in your family, then good for you.

What is the message you want to give your daughter about her working life? Make a note of it on page 288.

" *Your job is to give her the confidence to make choices that are right for her.* "

Girls' Schools Association, *Your Daughter*

What do we do about guilt?

" *Don't try and be a perfect mother – what a grim legacy that would be to your daughters. Making mistakes yourself and owning them gives your daughters permission to do the same.* "

Alison, mum of two grown-up daughters

It's not just working mums who feel guilty. I ask mums *and* dads at workshops to raise their hand if they feel parental guilt and most hands go up.

High-pressure competitive parenting is a breeding ground for guilt. Guilt comes from feeling that you're not good enough. Guilt comes from choosing to do something that you could have avoided, or believe you could have done better. Guilt is a critical voice in your head, a lurch in your stomach or a quickening of the heart. By-products of guilt include depression, exhaustion, idleness, rows and inconsistency. Guilt-ridden parents spend money on more stuff and treats for their children, and alcohol and chocolate for themselves.

I can't think of a single benefit that is gained through paying attention to guilt when it causes you to feel bad about your parenting. Very occasionally, a little bit of guilt can act as a prompt to change something for the better, but guilt is so damaging to mums that I don't want to promote it here.

If you are sick of guilt taking charge, then is it time to move on? Imagine what it would be like if guilt didn't rule. Look at the space it would create for something much more valuable for you and your daughter. What would you put in that space instead?

Getting rid of guilt starts with knowing where it is coming from. I call it the 'G-spot', and you need to find yours! I know where mine is. For me, it feels like a buzzing in my stomach, and it buzzes when a daughter says 'I'm hungry' or 'I need my top but it's in the wash', or when I am running a workshop about daughters and missing my own daughter's school show.

A mum's advice on guilt

66 My number one tip would be to enjoy your own life – do things that give you pleasure and talk to your daughters positively about the things you love (including them)! Nobody wants a martyr for a mother (voice of experience). I talk to my daughters about why I love my job and how it makes me feel. Why it is important for me to develop strong relationships with my husband (their dad) and my friends. I do not want them to feel guilty about the decisions they make in their lives, so as much as possible I try to model this behaviour to them. I also want them to understand that you need to work at building relationships and cannot just take them for granted. I have made a pact with my sister to STOP FEELING GUILTY! We are much happier and our daughters will hopefully benefit from this. 99

Kate, mum of three daughters aged five, seven and nine

I am including Kate's advice because I think she makes some great points about being a role model and not letting guilt rule as follows:

- Her number one tip is to enjoy your own life so that you can talk positively about the things you love to your daughters. This kind of passion and enthusiasm is great modelling, and creates a mum who is much more intriguing and attractive than a 'martyr' mum.
- She explains to her daughters why she loves her job and how it makes her feel. Much better for your daughter to hear this than work grumbles. At the same time, not everyone has a job they love, but wherever possible talk about the benefits of working instead of focusing on the negatives.
- She makes it very clear to her daughters that relationships take effort and nurturing, and not to take them for granted.
- She sees the damage guilt does and has taken action with her sister to banish guilt.

Where is your G-spot? Make a note of it.
Paying attention to guilt wrecks our confidence. Don't let guilt have the power to drive your actions. Concentrate on how most of the time you are doing your best, you love your daughter and you are not a saint. Make a note at the back of the book of five things you are doing that demonstrate you're doing what you can when you can out of love for your daughter. It is often the small, simple and free ideas that are the best.

One mum felt guilty about being unable to pick up her daughter from school. She texted her to say she would have to walk home. Instead of feeling guilty, she decided to focus instead on the exercise benefits to her daughter of a walk after school.

That's all I want to say about guilt – it doesn't deserve any more ink.

> *❝ I admire the mums who acknowledge their limits/weaknesses without becoming overwhelmed by them; those who do what they can and don't feel guilty about what they can't. ❞*
>
> Suzi, mum of a daughter 14 and a son 11

What would Marmar do?

 Writing about Marmar as a role model is a slightly mixed blessing. Her strengths were also her weaknesses. Her disinterest in timekeeping could also be seen as her gift of patience. Having little interest in her appearance meant she could spend half a day in her dressing gown regardless of who came to the house. I'm convinced there must be a link between staying in your dressing gown and being a relaxed mum! Her calm and optimistic disposition could go too far, like the time we told her a friend had died, and she said, 'Oh, I don't think so.'

She taught me the importance of being daft when parenting can be too serious. She showed us the value of rhymes and nonsense songs to get round the frustration of nappy changing or settling a child to sleep. Her mothering was full of small acts of kindness that usually cost nothing.

A few that I recall are her helping my sister and I to make a far bigger snowman than we could have managed on our own. On a hot summer's night, she dragged our beds and mattresses into the garden so we could sleep under the stars. As a teenager, she helped me make a white nylon jacket to wear to a David Essex (him again) concert. She would turn up to finish my babysitting jobs so I could go home to bed. As an adult, she would visit me at work or bring flowers to my flat. The flowers were always picked from her garden.

Marmar's visits to family, friends and neighbours meant that those home-grown posies popped up all over North London and beyond.

At the birth of each of my daughters, it was Marmar's garden posy that I kept beside my hospital bed. They would have been the first flowers their newborn eyes focused on. My sisters, and all her grandchildren remember countless small acts of kindness that she gave with love over her lifetime. The effects of which rippled far and wide.

While Marmar taught all her grandchildren many things, these are the things that her granddaughters treasured most when we were talking about Marmar after she died. (She taught many things to her grandsons as well – I will save their stories for a book about sons!)

She taught me how to arrange flowers.

Eleanor, aged 11

She showed me how to wear a necklace by looping it round twice.

Rosie, aged 13

> *" She taught me the importance of silliness and fun. And correct grammar. "*

Tilly, aged 18

> *" She made me a personalised duvet cover by hand, the entire thing by hand. "*

Marie, aged 30

> *" The over-riding memory I have of her is that she listened to me. "*

Phoebe, aged 21

Who are the Marmars in your life?

 Marmar was by no means a perfect mother. I am aware from the stories of many women I know or work with how painful and damaging a poor relationship with your mother can be. Your mum can be the last person you would want your own daughter to be influenced by. In families where there are relationship wounds across generations it's hard to know what to say when children inevitably ask questions about why they don't see their grandparents. If you are in this situation, there is extra support in the Directory.

However, if you want to take a moment to consider what your own mum, or other women from a different generation have meant to you, make some notes about whom these women are and what they offer you and your daughter.

What are you taking away from the fifth secret? Make some notes at the back of the book, preferably with your feet up and your favourite drink.

Mums:

Ditch the guilt - be the role model
you want her to have.

REMINDER

Take out of this secret what you feel is right for you and your daughter.

SECRET 6:
BUILD YOUR VILLAGE

CREATE A COMMUNITY TO HELP YOU AND YOUR DAUGHTER

Discover the secrets of:
- The value of the village.
- Build *her* village – who do you want around her?
- Build *your* village – who do you want around you?
- The village school – why it matters.
- Your village voice – why it's great to be nosy.

" *We're all in the same boat; surround yourself with supportive friends who understand without judging; learn that everyone else's daughters are not perfect!* "

Suzi, mum of a daughter aged 14 and a son

It takes a village to raise a child.

This saying, believed to have originated in Nigeria, has turned out to be what I have needed most to raise my daughters. I don't mean this to be an actual village. My village is a wider community of family, friends and neighbours that have been the biggest asset in keeping me going as a parent, especially when I felt I couldn't cope. Bumping into a neighbour, texting a mate, sharing concerns with my sister or having a moan to Marmar have all helped me move beyond the problem in front of me. And it was not only parenting problems. These kind souls have provided help and inspiration at home and in our neighbourhood when needed. The solid input of the community that has helped us to inspire, entertain and raise our children has given all of us strength and hope.

We have held each other's hands, laughed and cried over meals from fish fingers to feasts. Resources from baby stuff to ballet shoes, pasta recipes and parenting tips have been shared. My mothering of my daughters would have been parched and cracked without my community, or my village as I prefer to call it. My husband has also had the benefit of a host of men and women with whom to share the delights, dangers and puzzles of parenting.

Our daughters would not be the young women they are today without growing up among such a great collection of people who breathed life into them, especially when we couldn't.

66 *As a child, I loved visiting my mum's friend who would squeeze the life out of us, and give us cake – not something on offer at home.* 99

Emily, in her mid-thirties

Why is the village so important?

I believe that raising daughters among a supportive village community of family, friends and neighbours is a lifeline for parents and daughters (and sons), which is why it had to be my sixth secret. There are reasons though for cheering on the village.

- Many parents that I work with tell me that they feel cut off from family support. This is partly a casualty of our mobile population that can take us all over the world for love or for work. It is also because having children later in life automatically reduces the chances that our parents will be fit and able to help with childcare. It's more likely that we will need to help them, which is not easy should they live many miles away.

- Many parents find it hard to ask for help. We don't want to give away clues that we're finding parenting tough. Besides, parenting is supposed to come naturally isn't it? Your village understands parenting is tough and when you are honest about that and share the load, parenting daughters becomes easier and better for everybody.

> *" Make sure she has some adult 'champions' who believe in her, and enlist their help if you come up against a problem. "*
>
> Carla, mum of two grown-up daughters

A neighbour's 15-year-old daughter was desperate to go to a party. Information in the lead up to the party was patchy: the address kept changing, which parents would be there was uncertain and the details of any alcohol provision and finishing time were not forthcoming. Nothing too unusual for a teenage party, but as the families had known each other since their daughters were two and they knew most of the teenagers going, the parent's anxieties were low. The village will hope the party goes well, but if something does go wrong the learning is shared as well as the cleaning up! Next time there is a party, the parents and the teenagers will benefit from lessons learnt, such as having more adults at the party or making sure everyone knows the time of the last bus home.

Maybe you're already fortunate to be in your own supportive village, but could it be better? Let's see what it takes to build a great one in which to raise your daughter.

What do we want in a village?

" *My friends were so important in keeping me sane when the girls were little. We know we can have a good time together, but being there for each other during the difficult patches is when you really know who your friends are.* "

Elizabeth, mum of three teenage daughters

A vibrant village community is supportive, fun and life giving to its inhabitants. It creates a wider sense of 'home', giving us the confidence to venture out into the world and to look forward to returning. Your village might consist of people on your doorstep, but when I think of my village it includes people from all over the world. It's a network of all ages and types of characters who inspire and educate the younger members into adulthood. Human beings aren't designed to live in isolation, nor rear their young that way. It's expecting too much of parents to bring up children without support, as any single parent knows. When we pool our resources we have a lot to offer each other and our children. A village is greater than the sum of its parts – the benefits are sometimes hard to put your finger on, but that mystery is part of the gain that comes from being among people who can share your values.

Our darling daughters benefit from other people of different ages and outlooks to help them into womanhood. My girls have thrived on knowing all kinds of women and men, not just family members. These gifted grown-ups have listened to them; taught them skills like how to sew a hem, polish a CV, play a card game or tackle maths homework; and provided childcare, outings or work experience. But these are not their greatest gifts – it is the time they have given to show their interest, to listen, to care and to share advice.

Girls don't need many good role models, but a caring auntie or uncle, godparent, neighbour or older friend can be such an asset as they work out who they are and what values are important to them.

> 66 *I admire my auntie and uncle –*
> *they're really fair to their kids.* 99
>
> Bella, aged 14

How to build a great village for *your* daughter

Let's start by asking who is already in her village? Make a list or draw a mind map on the notes pages of all the people your daughter is in contact with who are a good influence on her.

Next, look back to Secret 2 (pages 70–91). Are there some values you see in action by other people that would you like your daughter to absorb? Are any values missing in your village? Perhaps there is someone inspirational with values similar to your own who could show an interest in your daughter? It might be a woman, older or younger than her mum. It could be a man who, though very different to her dad, could expand your daughter's mind and build her heart and her vision of a decent man. If her dad or her mum isn't around, are there other trustworthy men or women that could spend time with your daughter?

I appreciate the process of thinking about who is (or isn't) there for your daughter can hurt if you have no extended family available or a good network of friends, but I hope you might use the following exercise as a way to build a village for her.

> 66 I admire my friend who has been bringing up her daughter on her own pretty much and always puts her daughter first even when she was going through separation from her husband. She still managed to have fun with her and give her the loving network of friends and family that she particularly needed during this difficult time for them both. 99
>
> Tessa, mum of two daughters

Ask yourself:
- Who is helping my daughter to grow up well, apart from us as her parents?
- Who loves her?
- Who shows an interest in her?
- Who listens to her?
- Who teaches her life skills?
- Who can she trust?
- Who is kind to her?
- Who encourages her?

Where are these village people?

> " *I'm grateful for my daughter's godmother; she is 55 and has raised two lovely daughters and she is a super godmother to my children; always there when she is needed for love and laughter.* "

Karen, mum of a daughter aged eight and a son

You may know your village people already, but they can be found in schools, charities and in religious communities or they may be neighbours, youth workers, activity or club leaders, older friends and siblings, employers, work experience providers or community volunteers. They could also be found online. There are websites (see page 254) that can help your daughter access help and wisdom.

> " *I admire my friend's mum, she's mother to us all really, but also a great friend. She's completely non-judgemental and is always up for laughing with us as well as being ready with a hug when we need one!* "

Issy, aged 20

People in your village can provide a different perspective from yours, but sometimes that is a good thing especially when your daughter is in her teens and is naturally inclined to experiment or rebel against her parents' values.

" *Develop extended family relationships so she has someone else, rather than just you, to talk to. Trust her judgement, and remember her choices are her choices not yours.* "

Jules, mum of two teenage daughters

Next, think about who your daughter would include on her own list or mind map. It might be the famous faces she plasters over her bedroom wall or watches on YouTube, but be curious about her role models rather than critical. Ask her:

Who are her role models?
Who inspires her? Friends, family, neighbours or famous people?
Who does she trust?
Who does she learn from?

If this feels like too many questions, you could simply ask her:

Which adults do you admire and why?

In speaking to daughters for this book, they offered up a selection of ideas of whose parenting skills they rate.

" *I admire my nana because she managed to raise three kids in a foreign country on her own. She is also a great listener and always willing to give me advice.* "

Gemma, aged 18

" I admired my friend's mum growing up because she was easy to talk to and trusted me. "

Laura, aged 21

" My friend's mum allows her daughter to have alcohol at home every once in a while so that she learns to drink responsibly. This is better than drinking in front of her and telling her that she can't have any, which may result in sneaking out and drinking herself silly at a friend's house. She also talks openly about sex and what she can and can't do when she is in a relationship. This is really important because girls often become 'blinded with love', despite the guy not being too good for her. Knowing how and where to set the boundaries is key. "

Amy, aged 15

" The Queen is a nice nanny and mummy. "

Ella, aged seven

" Lily Allen. Although she is famous, she is down to earth and does everything with her daughter herself. "

Ruby, aged 17

The village idiots

Pardon the label, but needs must. Friendships are such a large part of your daughter's world, and sadly there could be some in her village who are a threat to her happiness. Parents are understandably concerned about unsuitable friends like those mentioned in Secret 3 – the Veruca Salts of the world. Bitchy girls cause havoc and wreck self-esteem with their comments, rumour spreading or physical abuse. The different rules that operate in other families – allowing late nights and answering back, for example – will influence your daughter who may bring these behaviours into your home.

Dealing with what's allowed, or not, in other village families is frustrating, and as unpredictable as the British weather. These external influences leak into your home and challenge your family's values that you're trying to instil into your daughter.

I caught up with a friend recently who has teenagers and two children under ten. She was commenting on how her younger children's friends are allowed more freedom than her teenagers' group were at the same age. Over just a few short years, she felt that parents had allowed more precocious or pushy behaviour, bad or cheeky language, and exposure to adult concepts through unsuitable films, TV programmes and computer games. It takes courage to hold your nerve and be the unpopular parent with stricter rules than your daughter would like. It is not our job to make our children happy all the time. It is our job to acknowledge their disappointment, without bending the family rules. Here are some tips to help you respond.

TIPS

- Recognise that how other families live their lives can be fascinating, exciting and intriguing to your daughter.

- Homes where there is little or no parental supervision can be the preferred location for teenagers to gather, but don't bow to pressure to relax the rules in your house, nor be reluctant to find out what supervision is on offer.
- If your daughter is comparing your family unfavourably to her friend Poppy's, you could say you expect that she wishes you were more like Poppy's family.
- Explain to her that you understand she's upset that you have certain house rules (unlike at Poppy's house), but that you believe your decision on phones in bedrooms at night, for example, is the right one. She needs her sleep.
- Use the 'In our house we…' (For example, 'In our house we switch phones off during meal times.'), using simple clear friendly communication instead of stern warnings or long lectures.
- At the same time, rules need refreshing as your daughter grows up and circumstances change, or they could be relaxed for a special occasion.
- Be welcoming to friends. Offer tea and toast, a listening ear and a lift home if you can.

Diversions from 'unsuitable friends'

There were some kids in my wider circle of teenage friends whom my dad bluntly called 'a bunch of no-hopers'. Kids who smoked, drank cider, bunked off school and were up for some petty crime. I resented Dad's objection to my 'exciting friends', but without admitting it I also knew he was right. It was a phase I went through, and what inspired me to turn away from the 'no-hopers' was getting a Saturday job. It was in a florist's and the owners and staff were creative, hard working and encouraging. Just the kind of people my 17-year-old self needed to meet. Although they were very different, my parents grew to love the florists and they knew I was in good hands when I was at the shop. I still see the florist owners 40 years later and think of them now as my 'village elders', especially after the death of my parents. The diversion of a Saturday job was a good outcome for me, and here are some other ideas that can be positive diversions for your daughter.

TIPS

- Recognise that in your daughter's teen years when she is experimenting and working out who she is, it is normal for her to be attracted to all sorts of people. 'Unsuitable friends' may be a phase she goes through, so don't panic too soon.
- Keep her busy, but not too busy. Support her to start or maintain hobbies or interests.
- Find her volunteering opportunities in your village that will give her experience and increase her chances of finding paid work.
- Help her find babysitting, dog walking, car cleaning or gardening jobs.
- Keep a list of chores that you're happy to pay her do to.
- Ask family, friends or godparents if they would be willing to spend some time with her.
- Spend time with her yourself (perhaps visiting a gallery or museum or engaging in a sport) or put something in the diary that you both can look forward to.

Neighbours

Opposite my childhood home was an open grass space that was like a village green. On the green, we played freely with neighbours' children without adult supervision, yet within sight of any parent who looked out of a window. We knew all the families that lived round the green and we were fed, told off and looked after by all of them. If we had set up a time lapse camera on the green during the 1970s it would have revealed footage of happy, growing children playing chase and football, leapfrogging, perfecting handstands and cartwheels and having snowball fights, followed by glimpses of kiss chase (chasing and then kissing whoever you catch) and teenage girls sunbathing in bikinis.

Parents today often describe to me what they valued most about their childhood was being free to play outside for hours, finally coming home worn out, hungry and grubby. They reflect on how they miss being able to give this freedom to their children. Their daughters are too busy with little spare time, or they worry that their daughters will be hurt or even abducted. They're not sure whom to trust. Parents find it sad and frustrating to acknowledge the gap between the strong parent-filled community that allowed them childhood freedom and the protected, scheduled life of supervised and paid-for childcare of their daughters.

A parent's village story

❝ *Last year we were at a tricky stage with our 15-year-old daughter Lily... Lily was becoming much more of a handful and we didn't like Ruby witnessing all the arguments, door slamming and rudeness from her big sister. We booked a two-week holiday in the summer, and Lily moaned about being 'stuck with us losers in some boring cottage'. She begged us to let her come for half of the holiday so she could do some school work at home alone. We did understand that this kind of holiday could be boring for Lily and she could not ask a friend along as there was no room. At the same time, we didn't feel ready to leave her home alone. We explained this to her, and we agreed we would see what we could do. I had a chat with my neighbour about it, and she said she was also having a problem over the summer finding enough childcare to cover her working days. She wondered if Lily would be up for some childcare, and we ended up with Lily going to stay with them for a week and then coming down to join us for a week in the 'boring cottage'. It was a great answer to a string of problems made possible by good neighbours. Phew!* 99

Ali and Jim, parents of Ruby aged nine and Lily aged 15

I am including Ali and Jim's story because it's such a positive example of the village in action, which can be especially welcome during the teen years. What I particularly like about Ali and Jim's actions are that they did take Lily's needs and feelings seriously instead of just dragging her along on the holiday. This meant they could find ways forward that worked for all of them and minimised the risk of her moods and behaviour spoiling a much-needed family holiday.

Notice how:

- They were honest about how bad Lily's behaviour was becoming and the effect this was having on their younger daughter and their holiday plans. Being truthful about what's happening and how it makes you feel is always the best place to start.
- They had a proper chat with Lily and listened to her and how she felt. They said they understood how this holiday could be boring for her. They had the imagination to see it was important to have

some flexibility. They also offered to see what could be done without making empty promises that they couldn't keep.

- They shared their story with their neighbour, and in doing so discovered that she was looking for childcare, which meant they could solve each other's needs. Since the summer, Lily has carried on babysitting for the neighbours for an hour before school so the parents don't have to take their toddler on the school run. Lily enjoys earning regular money and having another reason (apart from school) to get up and out of the house on time.

You might not have a 'village green', but I believe there is great value in growing relationships with neighbours to share the parenting load. Your neighbours might not be people who you would choose as friends, but your friends were strangers once too. Surely it's worth investing in building good relationships with each other for your children's sake if nothing else? Sadly when neighbours don't get on, I have seen how stressful it can be. If this is your situation, I hope you are able to resolve it even if it means mediation to find the peace that everyone needs in and around his or her home.

> Growing and nurturing your unique relationships with your neighbours is the secret of a happy village.

How do you grow good relationships with your neighbours? Try being a nosy neighbour. I don't mean a nuisance, but a neighbour that actively shows an interest, listens and is there for a cup of sugar, to feed the cat or to care for a child.

Even if you have lived among your neighbours for years and don't know them, there are two occasions when you can start being 'nosy'. One is at Christmas time when, in the spirit of 'Peace on Earth and goodwill to all men', you can invite the neighbours round. If providing food and drinks is difficult, suggest everyone brings something to share. I have seen Christmas drinks lead to summer barbeques and street parties. A social event completely changes how you then chat to each other in the street. This growing friendship and trust in each other will, of course, be witnessed by your daughter.

> " *I decided to invite the other people in the flats on my stairs round for a Christmas drink. I was nervous and it was a bit awkward to start with, but everyone enjoyed it and now when we meet on the landing we talk instead of ignoring each other.* "

Jackie, mum of a daughter aged ten

The other time when it is easier to be a nosy neighbour is when somebody new moves into the area. It gives you the chance to be welcoming and to introduce yourself and offer some local tips. When a neighbourhood feels like an extension of home, everyone benefits.

> " *Although we live in a big city and don't know many neighbours, the local church is a brilliant place as they are a community centre for everyone to use every day, not just for Sunday services. They organise a great spring fair, with a barbeque, music, bouncy castles and a fabulous range of stalls selling delicious cakes, plants, good quality bric-a-brac and vintage clothes, not the usual junk at all. My kids love it. This year the*

vicar asked everyone to sing 'Happy Birthday' to a lady called Tilly who was 100 that day. My daughter is called Tilly too, and I have a photo of my six-year-old Tilly with 100-year-old Tilly. There's something special about my Tilly connecting with someone at the opposite end of her life, especially as our parents live hours away. The church fair helps my kids meet all sorts of people and glues the neighbourhood together. My 12-year-old has been asked to help out on the tombola next year – that will help her maths skills! **"**

Laura, mum of two daughters

I am including Laura's story because it is a delightful example of the unexpected gains from being involved in your village. Laura demonstrates her willingness to enable her daughters to gain from their village as follows:

- She's up for trying different things on offer locally. A church fair might have a musty reputation, but she has given it a go and discovered it's great and her daughters love it too - a fun, local outing for all of them.
- She can see that meeting a variety of local people of all ages and backgrounds enriches her daughters' lives.
- It will provide her older daughter with an introduction to volunteering and taking responsibility by helping out on the tombola stall.

Build a great village for *you*

My neighbours have been a vital part of my village and they have helped me raise my daughters. We trust each other to look after each other's children, we swap house keys and we take each other's bins out. We have celebrated birthdays and New Year's Eve together. We have shared the joy of babies being born, watched our children grow up and leave, and the sadness of loved ones dying. Just after my dad died, my daughter opened the front door to go to school and found a candle burning in a jam jar, with a card and flowers from a caring neighbour.

Beyond my neighbours there are others living in the four corners of the world who I consider to be in my village. Sometimes we take each other for granted and it can take someone, like my friend Linda who died from breast cancer when she was just 44, departing too soon for us to appreciate what our village means to us.

To build and sustain a village of support for you, I have some questions for you that are very similar to the ones you considered for your daughter.

While I appreciate the value of online networks for support and advice, I believe nothing replaces human contact!

These are delicate questions. Take care as you consider them and forgive me if they are a sad reminder of those now absent from your village. Remember your answers can include anyone, not just those in your neighbourhood. Write your answers on page 289.

Who loves you?
Who shows an interest in you?
Who listens to you?
Who do you trust?
Who is kind to you?
Who encourages you?
Who offers you practical help?
Who do you need in your village?
What will you do to grow your village?

Tips to grow your village

- Be generous – you'll get out what you put in.
- Be trustworthy, not a gossip.
- Be friendly – invite people round, meet them for a drink or in the park.
- Start a new hobby or take up a sport.
- Suggest a play date.
- Join or set up a babysitting circle.
- Be helpful – offer to run an errand or visit someone who is lonely. .
- Volunteer at nurseries, schools, Cubs, Scouts, Brownies and Guides or other children's clubs. Contact your local council for a list of volunteering opportunities.
- Organise or go to a charity fundraising event.
- Join or start a litter pick up in the park or on your street.
- Plan a street party – do a leaflet drop to see who wants to help organise.

The village school

Whether your daughter's school is a five-minute walk or she's boarding five hours away, it's part of your village. She spends so much of her time at school, it's important to be involved if you can. You will get a clearer picture of what the school is really like and spend time getting to know her darling friends!

My daughters went to several schools as we moved cities, and we all had to start again making new friends. Helping out at their schools, even two hours once a month, made the transition more bearable. Most nurseries and schools are usually very grateful for extra pairs of hands. During the secondary school years, your independent daughter is likely to want to keep you away from school as much as possible, but investigate the parents' association or try to assist with school shows or sports events.

If you can, support the parents' association to raise money for the extra equipment that cash-strapped schools don't have. It's not just about money though. Social events in schools help the village to thrive. Our school's parents association runs the bar at school concerts, sells second-hand uniforms and organises quiz nights and family sports events.

I would say it's worth a day off work to help out on a school trip. Instead of a day at work, you could be at a castle, gallery, zoo, museum or the theatre while holding small hands and chaperoning a crocodile of children.

> *" I signed up to help on my daughter's school ski trip. Twenty-four hours on a coach with excited 11-year-old girls was grim, but a week with my daughter and her class in the snow was brilliant. Next year, I guess I will be the last person she would want on a school trip. "*

Simon, dad of three teenage daughters

What kind of education do you want for your darling?
Forty years ago, I remember feeling really worried that I would disappoint my parents if I failed the exam to get into the girls' grammar school that my older sister attended. The difference today is the stress it creates in families to get places in the best schools, whereas my parents' generation were more content, or didn't have any other choice except to just go to the local school.

I could write at length about how to choose a school for your daughter, but I'd rather have a cup of tea with you and find out what *you* want for her from her education. I could point you towards the studies which come out saying girls perform better academically in girls' schools, but is school just for learning? Sometimes an all-girl school environment pumps up the pressure on girls to achieve an unrealistic set of exam results. A wise school cares for your daughter's happiness first, as that is what will help her learn best. When looking for a school, I would always recommend finding out what pastoral care is offered and how much this is prioritised over achieving academic excellence.

I believe going to a local school is the best way to be plugged into your village. Not easy if that school is the last place you would send your darling, and moving house is out of the question. The enormous lengths some parents go to secure places at schools creates toxic anxiety. I have met families who have registered a daughter for a particular school as soon as they know they are having a daughter. In some parts of the UK, the lack of places available in both state and private sector schools piles on the pressure for parents, which reverberates round the family. Girls as young as four can feel the burden to pass entrance exams. I wonder sometimes if having a range of schools to choose from creates more problems than it solves.

When we started our married life, my husband and I wanted a family, but we didn't have a conversation about what kind of education we would choose for our children. I have seen too many couples with divided opinions over this issue. If you have never really talked with your partner about schooling for your daughter, or if you're arguing about it, here are some tips to help you both work out your values and your plans for educating your daughter.

Our education wish list for our daughter

Ask yourselves these questions separately, and then compare your answers.

- What do you believe educating girls is for? (If you have sons too, this will illuminate if you have different gender beliefs about the purpose of education.)
- What are your best memories of school?

- What do you want from the schools where your daughter will spend 13 or so years of her life?
- What are the most important values that you want to find in action in the schools your daughter attends?
- What are your views on paying for education? Never? Maybe? Definitely?

Your answers will help you both to decide and agree on the most important factors to be considered when choosing a school for your daughter.

Education is more than school

A man named Dieudonne came to stay, a former African street child, who now runs a charity for street children. When Dieudonne was a boy, his father was murdered in Burundi's civil war. Overnight his family fell apart, and he was left on the streets.

Listening to Dieudonne tell his story was an education to appreciate what we take for granted – security, safety, a bed to sleep in and food on the table all provided with love.

We have tried to give our daughters as wide an education as possible, to expand their minds way beyond the school gate. We want them to grow up experiencing different people, places, art, science, nature, sport, food and entertainment and without spending a fortune.

It is what we want our legacy to our daughters to be. It's the parenting story we're trying to write.

If you believe you want education to be beyond the school gate for your daughters, can I ask you to return to your education wish list and add to it?

Outside of school, what is your educational legacy to your daughter?

Talk about this with your partner before writing up or drawing a mind map of your educational legacy list. Of all the things on your educational legacy list, what can you find in your village?

> *My friends have raised their daughter and their sons in the same gentle way. They have always treated them as fully-formed people, brimming with creativity and art and purpose.*

Kate, mum of a daughter aged five

MY FAVOURITE TIP

Parenting daughters: a life's work in progress made easy by the village.

What would Marmar do?

 Marmar trained as a schoolteacher, and was an advocate of sending your children to the nearest school. From ages five to 18, my sisters and I went to two schools, both less than five minutes' walk away. She couldn't understand why parents today go to great lengths to choose schools involving long school runs. She thought putting children into cars to go to school was madness. I sometimes wonder though if part of this came from her dread of mornings!

As her granddaughter Marie said:

> *When I was a child, Marmar was the only adult I knew who could sleep in so late.*

Our local community of neighbours and friends was like an extended family, as our blood relatives were on the other side of the world. Marmar was naturally 'nosy' and an unknowing expert on building a village. We grew up to a soundtrack of her chatting and giggling with neighbours, friends and strangers about anything from the weather to a missing cat. She could also be a listening ear on the phone or at the garden gate to concerns and conundrums, truly 'loving her neighbour as herself'. The downside to this meant she was often unintentionally late or dinners were burnt. She wasn't a typical post-war mother who found her identity in keeping house. She was her own special blend of feminist ideals and selflessness lived out in her own time zone.

Part of her legacy to me has been the value of being involved with your village on the doorstep and beyond. She lived with an open front door where all were welcome and offered tea. Meals were stretched to feed unexpected visitors. Long before email, she would write letters and cards to far away family and friends, usually starting them and finally posting them months later. But then, a thoughtful letter never arrives at the wrong time. Her warmth and kindness to others meant an all-age village turnout of over 300 people at her funeral – something that would have utterly amazed her.

What are you taking away from the sixth secret? Make some notes at the back of the book.

Build Your Village:
Create a community to help you and your daughter.

REMINDER
Take out of this secret what you feel is right for you and your daughter.

SECRET 7: PATIENCE

YOU ARE A PARENT FOREVER – THERE IS NO RUSH

> **"** I hope she remembers me as a patient,
> loving mum who she could talk to about almost
> everything and have a laugh with too. **"**

Sarah, mum of one daughter and a son

Discover the secrets of:
- The value of patience.
- The scrapbook - creating memories to last a lifetime.
- *7 Secrets of Raising Girls Every Parent Must Know* delivered and what are you taking away?
- Goodnight from Marmar.

The value of patience

Patience will give the parents with daughters exactly what they want. It will help you take a hope-filled longer view, which will reduce anxiety. It will also keep you in the moment, so that you don't miss out on what is actually happening now. It gives you the space in which to press the pause button and then the time so you can ask yourself: 'What is this about? How can I respond best to what is going on?'

Patience will deliver those parts of parenting that you love most. With patience, you will catch those darling daughter moments that can't be planned, like the first step or word, a spontaneous hug, a sloppy kiss or an overdue catch up with your teenager.

Patient parents see the value in walking at the pace of their toddler as she stops to pick up petals or examine an ant. Patient parents stay calm as their darling daughter hurls requests for immediate play dates or treats. Patient parents wait up for the teenager to come home safely, and wait for her fury to calm.

Patient parents are lovely to observe because they have the capacity to listen and engage with their daughters. How do they do it? Are they born that way or is patience something we can learn? I think it's both. Unlocking the secret of patience is a gift that I want to leave with you and your daughters.

> 66 *Whatever the behavioural struggle you're coming up against, be patient with yourself and with your daughter. This is a moment. In three months, you won't even remember this thing that is driving you crazy.* 99

Annie, mum of a daughter aged five and a son aged two

I have recently been coaching a mum of two small children. The summer holidays are looming and her greatest desire is to get through eight weeks of the school vacation without a summer of either losing her temper or counting the days to September. She said she would like to have 'a river of patience'. She described what a river of patience would give her: a flowing sense of calm, enabling her to manage all sorts of tensions that come from looking after small children for weeks on end. This river would let her float along at a gentle pace. It would give her that elusive patience needed to strap a child into a car seat or listen to a long-winded gripe.

Her metaphor of the river of patience reminded me of other situations where water brings calm to frazzled parents and their daughters. A bath, a swim, a long drink of cool water and even rain running down a window will soothe and rehydrate a tired body or mind.

Children know the pleasures of water instinctively. They giggle and splash in water for long stretches of time - bath time, paddling pools or at the beach. A friend of mine used to join her husband on work trips, which meant a lot of time cooped up in hotels all over the world with their two little daughters. When they were jet-lagged or cranky, she would put them in the bath, which kept them entertained for hours, even at 3.00 a.m.! If you have older daughters, you may be familiar with the lack of hot water remaining after girls have had their baths or showers.

Water may help calm things down, but there are a variety of tips in this final secret that will bring more patience into your parenting without the need to get wet!

It is important to recognise that although patience is deeply sought after, it can be very difficult to find.

> *Achieving patience is a greater miracle than raising the dead.*

St John of the Cross, a sixteenth-century friar

We may expect too much of patience, and it often features in something I call the 'If only' syndrome. Parents often say to me 'I would be a better parent *if only* I had…'

… more time.
… more money.
… more energy.
… a bigger house/garden.
… a better job.
… a partner who was kinder/listened.
… more patience!

TIP

Patient parent = patient daughter.

> *Think long term. Build her assertiveness and resilience and let her solve her own problems. To do this you will have to model assertiveness and resilience!*

Angie, mum of an 18-year-old daughter and a son

Part of the secret of patience means having the willpower to wait. It means being content and accepting that part of the solution to a problem is waiting and that there is nothing more you can do. Waiting to find out your daughter's exam results is a perfect example of this. Patience promotes lowering expectations in the first place. It means delayed gratification. It means being prepared to say 'No, not yet' to your daughter and showing her the value of doing the same.

Your daughter can be interested in acquiring a huge amount of *stuff now* thanks to clever marketing, a friend's influence or an indulgent family. You can ask your daughter to make a good case for what she wants and why, but you need to be sure of your position rather than being browbeaten into submission. If you're sure your answer is a 'no' and she already knows why, then 'no' is all you need to say. It's like being a stuck record. If your 'no' becomes a 'Yes, OK then' she is learning that pester power works.

I know that sticking to 'no' is good in theory, and in practice we're sometimes too tired and fed up to stick to our position. But I also know that a clear 'no' works! It might not make your daughter happy - being the cause of upsets is inevitable sometimes - and what helps her best is that she knows 'no' means 'no'.

I overheard this conversation recently between a dad and his teenage daughter:

> 66 Daughter: *Dad, I don't want my cousins coming over. Make Mum ring them up and say I'm out.*
>
> Dad: *No.*
>
> Daughter: *Dad, make her!*

> Dad: No.
>
> Daughter: *Dad, you're so mean, Mum won't listen. Just MAKE HER DO IT!*
>
> Dad: No.
>
> Daughter: *Why not? Pleeeeessssseeee! Just get her to phone them!*
>
> Dad: *We have already discussed this, and the answer is no.*
>
> Daughter: *That's so unfair.*
>
> Dad: *I can see you think it's unfair, and it's still a no.*
>
> *(Daughter grunts, and both dad and daughter are silent for a while.)*
>
> Dad: *I'm off to get a coffee, do you want one?*
>
> Daughter: No. **99**

I am including this snippet of eavesdropping, as I think it's a great example of a patient consistent parent saying 'no'.

- He kept his voice and tone relaxed and neutral, not sarcastic or patronising.

- He didn't get sucked in to giving her long explanations.
- He didn't appear to be affected by his daughter's increasing frustration and nagging.
- He used empathy when he said 'I can see you think it's unfair.'
- There wasn't a perfect happy ending where both were satisfied. Though the happy ending may sometimes be the outcome, the important thing here is that his daughter learnt that 'no' means 'no'.

Patience means working with what you have, rather than believing things will change for the better *if only* you had... Patience is something you can grow if you want to. And if you did that, ask yourself and your daughter, what would more patience give you?

TIP

Self-audit your patient and impatient trigger points.

- Accept that it is normal for parents to lose their patience, but don't let guilt rule when you do. Apologise and move on, without feeling the need to give your daughter a compensating treat.
- How are YOU? Self-care has popped up throughout *Darling Daughters*, but it's always worth repeating: parents who are tired, hungry, bored, hung-over and stressed will struggle to be patient. This is a final call for the value of looking after yourself in order for you to look after your daughter until she is at least 35.
- Impatience comes from being overwhelmed with too many or too high expectations, such as 'It's wrong to be late' or 'My daughter must have clean uniform.' Take the opposite view. Ask yourself what is the worst that could happen if she was late or went to school with porridge on her uniform?

- Over a week, keep a diary of what situations wind you up and make you more likely to lose your patience. Equally, note down when you have been patient. How did you do it?
- Who do you know who is patient? Interview them; ask how they do it.

How to grow patience

These tips can be shared with your daughter so that she too can grow patience.

- **Don't wear your watch** or carry other time-keeping devices from Friday night to Sunday night and when on holidays.
- **Leave blank slots in the diary** and write in 'do nothing' in these free times.
- **Engage with the outdoors**. In the short term, take a daily walk or give yourself a day out. For the longer term, plan a camping trip or a break that includes spending as much time as possible outdoors.
- **Take up a technology-free, slow hobby**. Gardening, reading for pleasure, jigsaw puzzles, knitting, sewing, bird watching, drawing and painting all require you to slow down and take your time. Bread making is another one I heard recently that helps you relax.
- **Consider a spiritual quest**. Those with an active faith talk about how it gives them patience. Yoga, meditation, mindfulness and prayer can help you let go, calm down, breathe better and worry less.
- **Breathing.** Notice how rapidly you breathe as your patience thins. Breathe in for seven counts, out for 11. You can do this anywhere – I do it when I'm stuck in traffic.

> " *We can only go forward in time, so to spend time dwelling on past events that went wrong, creates the wrong energy to go forward. Forgive yourself and others, know that you're just doing the best you can with the resources that you had in that moment.* "

Sarah, mum of three grown-up daughters
and a son, and Reiki practitioner

I hope these tips might be of use to you, but what tips have you got for growing patience? Send them to me at www.darlingdaughters.org.

Another easy way to grow patience is to reflect on what you're grateful for, rather than what you don't have. Gratitude removes the 'if only' syndrome and allows patience in. One of my favourite ways to grow gratitude has been to document my daughters' lives so far.

The scrapbook – creating memories to last a lifetime

> " *Take lots of photos and videos, as your children will forget and so will you probably. By recording it you will have permanent (cherished, hopefully!) memories.* "

Janet, mum of a daughter aged nine and a son aged 11

There is a gift industry out there to help you collect stories, photos and memorabilia to mark your daughter's milestones. You can keep her hair, her milk teeth, her first shoes and her teddy bear in specially designed containers. You don't need any of these special containers – any box will do the same job. You can imprint her baby hands or feet into ceramic or precious metals to display at home alongside photos of her. She can star in hundreds of home movies to be enjoyed at family film nights for the rest of her life.

When my daughters were little the things I particularly loved were the funny things they said, so I started to write them down. I was concerned I would forget them, and that as their verbal skills grew their quirky questions, like 'Do the stars have birthdays?', and daft comments would diminish. One afternoon we were driving past Toys R Us when our eldest (aged three at the time) piped up from the back seat, 'That should be "Toys We Are".' There were also the inevitable wee and poo jokes and the made up words. In our family, an apricot is called a 'choose wisely'. I was explaining to my middle daughter that not all the apricots in the fruit bowl were ripe, so choose wisely, at which point my youngest, aged three at the time, said 'Can I have a choose wisely Mummy?'

To mark their eighteenth birthdays, I have given each of my girls a scrapbook containing photos from zero to eighteen, sprinkled with their funny sayings, along with snippets of their handwriting and some drawings. Making up their scrapbooks felt like a hilarious and tearful ride in a time machine. A stark reminder of how fast the years had flown between my pregnancy to my 18-year-old daughter on the brink of leaving home. A friend of mine has written a letter to each of her daughters every year on their birthdays, describing her feelings for them and what the year had been like. These touching letters were read out at their eighteenth birthday celebrations.

> *It is hard realising that (at last) the eldest has her own life now she's away at university, and being OK with not thinking/worrying about her every day.*

Tom, dad of three daughters aged 13, 17 and 20

View-Master moments

Alongside the scrapbooks, photos, videos and other keepsakes, there have also been hundreds of what I think of as View-Master moments. A View-Master is a toy into which you insert discs of images. While looking through the binocular-like lenses you click the shutter to move through all the images on the disc. In my youth View-Master discs had images of famous landmarks, such as the Eiffel Tower, *click*, the Taj Mahal, *click*, Sydney Opera House, *click*, Big Ben and so on. As my daughters have grown up my View-Master moments are those that I couldn't anticipate let alone have a camera to hand and which are now freeze framed in my mind. My View-Master moments are an assortment of images, sounds, smells and touches.

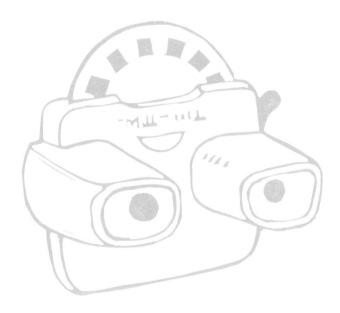

I can picture in my mind each daughter being pushed in her buggy, going off to school, asleep in bed, watching TV or doing homework. I can still hear the faint sound of their baby breath. Hours of singing nursery rhymes and counting songs, before they moved on to 'The Sound of Music', a host of Disney melodies and then The Spice Girls took over. I could hear them brushing their teeth and braces to Radio 1 during their teen years, although by then music mainly entered their pierced ears via headphones. Bedroom doors were slammed after arguments, or from chasing one another cackling with laughter.

I can recall the smell of their newborn skin, soft as the finest suede. There have been countless times when I felt their little squidgy hands in mine long before they were adorned with rings and nail varnish.

I can feel their silky hair, too slippery for a ponytail, and smell the washing powder on their laundered clothes. The relief of being woken up by the smell of toast at 3.00 a.m. signalling that they were safely home after a night on the town.

Though unlikely to be of interest to anyone else, my View-Master moments are as precious to me as the photos and home videos.

> *I love it when she's happy to be a little girl again and cuddles on the settee with me. She asked me last week if I would mind drying her hair for her. (I've not been asked to do this in years.) I acted quite casual when I was doing it, but inside I was dancing for joy that she had asked me. I couldn't show too much excitement though!*

Rachel, mum of a daughter aged 16

It's never too late to start collating the memories you have of your daughter growing up. They are a significant part of your parenting story. If you haven't kept anything (or you can't remember!), ask other family or friends what they remember of her earlier years. When your daughter reaches 18 (or if she's past 18), what would you like to put in her scrapbook?

What about your View-Master moments? Those very ordinary memories of her life so far that will be unique to her and treasured by you. You might like to record them somehow so they are there for both of you to share in the future like a favourite story read over and over again.

Look back at what you have been through and how things that worried you at the time worked out in the end. I hope you find it heart-warming to recall the better memories than the times of sadness, anxiety, frustration and anger. There have been plenty of those too in raising my daughters, which out of respect for them are not described here, but believe me we have all had oceans of tears and tantrums and I guess more to come.

Today I'm writing this in a cafe and nearby is a mum with her little daughter who is probably under three. They are sharing a snack and chatting. 'It's mummy and daughter day; it's nice spending time with just you,' says the mum with a warm smile.

I'm reminded of the thousands of 'mummy and daughter days' I have been through to get to this point. As I said at the start of this book, I believe parenting is a life's work in progress. The intention of this book has been to help you find or simplify your own parenting road map based on your values and your legacy to your daughter. To give her a warm and loving backdrop to her childhood years, not distracted by stress, pressure, anxieties, panic and guilt. A home from which she is ready to leap, equipped to thrive on her own.

> *" It's hard letting them go and truly realising they are adults, but it's great they communicate now without the eye-rolling thing. "*

Helen, mum of two daughters aged 14 and 21

You'll probably wave and smile when the time comes for her to fly the nest, but your heart will be heavy from a mixture of pride and sadness. A daughter feeling free and ready to go means you have done a great job raising her. It also means she is more likely to come home and see you because she wants to, not because she feels she should. My grown-up daughters know they can always come home and I'm so delighted when they do.

> *" Mum always says this is your house, no matter what you can always come back home. I love that, even though I am a very independent woman, this makes me feel secure. "*

Lucy, aged 32

7 Secrets of Raising Girls Every Parent Must Know delivered
Reflecting on your own story of raising your daughter is part of the seventh secret, and it is the right note on which to end this book. Can I ask you to find a few minutes, make your favourite drink and then to look back over the book and the notes you have written?

> *It won't always be easy and you can be sure that she'll scream at you lots as a teen, but don't let that make you think you're not doing an awesome job. :)*

Ellie, aged 18

I hope you have found my secrets helpful. They are born from my failings, my joys and what I have learnt so far, combined with the voices of others. Most of all, I hope that you have found comfort and relief in hearing how normal it is to find parenting daughters a challenge and a mystery. 'Parenting' has rightly become a new verb instead of just a noun as it was in our parents' day. The art, the science, the joy and the mystery of our actions and our words make all the difference to our darling daughters, so please don't let guilt wreck your potential. The story of your parenting can be a fantastic read. In your lifetime you have a unique and rewarding opportunity, for which you will need the patience of a saint, to leave your darling daughter with a treasure chest of values to live her life by. Good luck.

> *I hope they'll remember me as someone who loved them unreservedly and who helped them to believe that they could make the world a better place and that I taught them that women can change the world.*

Sarah, mum of two daughters aged 12 and 14

Summary

Here are the secrets again for you, followed by a brief summary of each one.

Secret 1: Change

Understand and prepare for how your darling daughter grows up.

Whatever you do as a parent, your daughter will grow up thanks to an inbuilt set of instructions from Mother Nature. Knowing the essential points about her physical, mental and emotional development brings relief to parents who are wondering how to tackle challenges *and* make the most of each stage. A little girl with a new sibling might be fine with the baby, but suddenly become a handful for you. A daughter in her early teens being unkind to her mum is partly caused by hormone surges she's experiencing and partly because it's time for her to start separating from her family. Secret 1 is like a biology lesson that will help you know what to expect during the five stages of growing up, from birth to leaving home, and crucially what she needs at each stage from her mum and dad.

Secret 2: Values

Live by your legacy to your daughter.

When you're old and grey, you will have time on your hands to think back over the years of raising your daughter. You'll trawl through your memories of her, from the day she was born through her childhood and into adulthood. It's like reading the story of your parenting. Does it have a happy ending? What are your hopes for your daughter? Amid the distractions of daily life, we lose sight of what really matters to us, what we want in our story. Your biggest legacy to your daughter is a moral code, a set of values she can live her life by long after you've gone. It's never too late to decide what your values are as a parent and to start writing the story you will want to read and pass on. If today was your last day as her parent, what would you want to leave her with so she can grow up strong, loving and capable?

Secret 3: V-signs

Know what is essential to keep your daughter safe and happy

Never before have parents been more worried about their daughters! Girls, too, are buckling under the strain, trying to deal with being a modern girl in a fast-moving world. This secret is a guide to the main areas that concern parents of daughters, along with ideas that help you know what to do.

I call the concerns the V-signs:

V is for Virtual – she's online, help!

V is for Violins – the pressure she is under to achieve; from getting into the right school, having the right friends, passing violin exams and all the while looking stunning.

V is for Veruca Salt, the meanest girl in Roald Dahl's *Charlie and the Chocolate Factory* – the murky world of friendships and bullying, online and face-to-face.

V is for Vomit and Vaginas – from Calpol and nits through to periods and hangovers, her body is a minefield of pain and pleasure. A toddler fiddling with her 'front bottom' is the start of discovering sexual feelings that will be fully explored in her teens. Her initial experience of alcohol or other drugs could be rewarding enough for her to want some more. The pressure that your daughter may feel to look like a celebrity and behave like a porn star, to experiment with mind-altering substances or to resort to self-harm needs careful handling by anxious parents. Even if you have no particular worries at the moment, I hope you will see the value in reading through the V-signs to discover what might be coming your way.

Secret 4: Dads

Use your power wisely

Many dads I have talked to scratch their heads and wonder if they're only a walking wallet, chauffeur and spider catcher. They want to be more involved with their kids than their own dads were, but they are not sure where to start, and sometimes mums make it worse by criticising their efforts. All this can leave a dad feeling useless. But the opposite is true. A dad is important in his daughter's life from the moment she is created. You have great power to build her mind, her heart and her wish list for what to look for in a partner. Secret 4 shows you what she needs most from you and it will give you a set of tools so you can build a respectful and treasured relationship of unique value to you and your daughter.

Secret 5: Mums

Ditch the guilt – be the role model you want your daughter to have

The biggest influence on how a daughter turns out is her mum. The pressure this creates to be good role models to our daughters can slide into a toxic sewage of guilt and stress that drowns out the potential we have to be great role models. The message of Secret 5 is ditch the guilt. Tell guilt where to go. Guilt is such a waste of time and energy. Instead, Secret 5 invites you to refocus and be the role model you want to be instead of the one you think you should be. Forget the Penelope Perfect mums who knock your confidence and move on from the Moaning Milly mums. Drop the standards, increase the fun and recognise you're a human being not a saint. Our darling daughters are taking note of how we combine work and motherhood. What is the message we want to pass on to them about being career women, working mums or stay-at-home mums?

Secret 6: Build your village

Create a community to help you and your daughter

I believe raising daughters among a supportive 'village' community of family, friends and neighbours is the greatest lifeline for parents and daughters (and sons), which is why it had to be my sixth secret. I call it 'the village'. It is populated by the angels and heroes who live on your doorstep, but it could also include people who you love and admire but live far away.

Frequently parents confess feelings of sadness and isolation that are due to their wider family being too far away or unable to offer help. They also struggle to own up that they are finding it tough to raise children when everyone around them seems to be managing fine. A supportive village lowers the pressures and celebrates the milestones. Daughters need a variety of good role models to lift them into adulthood equipped with the life skills learnt from a kind auntie, neighbour or older friend. This is part of your daughter's education alongside the decisions you need to make about her schooling. Secret 6 also examines the value of supporting your daughter's education via the 'village school', which is a cornerstone of building a great village for you and your daughter.

Secret 7: Patience

You're a parent forever – there is no rush

Your daughter, like mine, will grow up in the blink of an eye and in no time she'll have left home. Days can drag, but years fly.

I also believe you're a parent until the day you die, so what's the rush? The clock dominates so much of modern parenting. What this does is pump up the stress. Combining that with a bewildering amount of choice in the developed world about everything from what to have for supper, which school to choose or where to buy shoes means it takes longer to reach decisions. Tension builds and we lose our patience. Parents are in such a rush they run the risk of missing the best bits - those bits that can't be planned for create the best memories - of raising their daughter.

A mum said to me, 'My impatience gets in the way of me being able to enjoy my daughter. Give me a river of patience.'

Patient parents are lovely to be around because they provide calm and have the capacity to listen and engage with their daughter. How do they do it? Are they born that way or is patience something we can learn? I think it's both. If you could be more patient, how would that make a difference to your parenting? Secret 7 takes the long view and offers you the gift of patience. For a daughter who wants everything *now*, learning the art of patience is no bad thing. This secret also looks at the value of being grateful for what you have by collecting memories of your daughter's life so far.

That's it, the seven secrets of raising a darling daughter, delivered in what I hope has been an enjoyable, useful and reassuring read.

Do share my secrets. I'm not just saying that to sell more books! You will know that you have really learnt something from this book when you find yourself explaining it to somebody else.

Share your thoughts with me too. Please write to me at www.darlingdaughters.org and leave all of us your best tips and stories for raising daughters. You will find more of Marmar's wit and wisdom there too, and an online Directory.

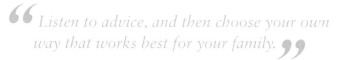

Listen to advice, and then choose your own way that works best for your family.

Anna, mum of a daughter aged ten and
two sons aged three and five

Goodnight from Marmar

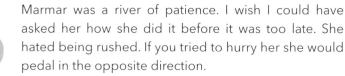

Marmar was a river of patience. I wish I could have asked her how she did it before it was too late. She hated being rushed. If you tried to hurry her she would pedal in the opposite direction.

She would say to me if I flew about in a flap, 'There is no rush.' It's a View-Master moment of her that I say out loud to remind me now to slow down.

As Alzheimer's grip tightened, we had to move Marmar out of our old family home and into a flat. During the months of clearing and sorting it became evident that the scrapbook idea had perhaps gone too far. It appeared she had kept *everything* from our childhood, even shipping it from one side of the world to the other. We found hand-knitted baby bootees and moth-eaten blankets, milk teeth and locks of hair, school books, drawings and cards all carefully packed away in a mountain of cardboard boxes piled up in our childhood bedrooms. Some of these treasures she had made more accessible for visiting grandchildren. They loved playing with our old toys, reading our Beatrix Potter books and wearing our 1970s clothes 30 years after we did.

Marmar was definitely a hoarder of good intentions. She kept things 'just in case' she or anyone else needed them. She couldn't bear to part with anything, including food well past its sell-by date. On top of a pile of Marmar's unsorted papers and miscellaneous junk we found a note in her handwriting. It said: 'Not to be thrown away,' which sums her up really.

Marmar didn't like change. She found leaving those she loved particularly difficult. Dad would say to her, 'I'll be in the car. You'll do anything but leave.'

As children, when she came in to say goodnight to us, she would sometimes whisper 'Night, night world' as if leaving us overnight meant her world was ending. When she did leave us for good, it felt as if our world did end for a while. The death of a parent causes you to question what his or her legacy to you is, and for me it was what kick-started this book. Marmar's wit and wisdom remain forever with me to hand on to my daughters and future generations. I hope you have found Marmar's part in this book a timeless reminder of what you received from your parents and how that might be important to you now and in the future as you raise your daughter. I would love to read your memories of your parents' legacy to you. Share them on the 'What would Marmar do?' page of www.darlingdaughters.org.

Marmar would love you to take your time to treasure the moments you have with your darling daughter. She would say to you, 'Don't worry, she'll be alright. Why don't you put your feet up and have forty winks?'

What are you taking away from the seventh secret? Make some notes at the back of the book.

Patience:

You are a parent forever – there is no rush.

REMINDER

Take out of this secret what you feel is right for you and your daughter.

RESOURCES

The final pages of this book contain these resources:

Directory (pages 253-265)
Lists of organisations, websites and helplines where you can find additional or specialised help. Some I have used myself, others have been recommended to me by others whose opinion I trust, but always do your own research. Please send your recommendations to www.darlingdaughters.org.

Book and Movie Club (pages 265-270)
Books and movies that contain good life lessons or strong female role models for your daughter. There is also a list of recommended parenting books.

Helpful handouts
Birth order (pages 270-273)
Birth order can make a difference to how your daughter grows up. This guide goes through the main features of each birth order position within the family and its associated characteristics.

How to learn to listen (pages 274-276)

Listening well to your daughter is one of the greatest gifts you can give her. It will also be the best way to help you understand her and know how best to help her.

Chores your daughter can do and when (pages 277-279)

Parents' Notes

Space in which you can record ideas and thoughts in any way you wish, and respond to questions.

Directory

Aren't we lucky to be only a click away from a world of advice and information that could help us to raise our darling daughters? But it can be confusing to know who and what to trust and for how long. In a fast-moving society, advice and information sources come and go overnight so please use these online resources as a springboard to what's out there at the moment. It might be useful to think of this material as the book's village notice board.

Below is a list of websites and books that were at the time of writing useful to parents and daughters. My intention is to keep the *Darling Daughters* Directory updated on the website, so if you come across something that you know will benefit all of us, do the *Darling Daughters* village a favour and get in touch at www.darlingdaughters.org.

How best to use the directory:

1. Make your favourite drink.
2. Put your feet up.
3. Trust your instincts – you know your daughter best.

Websites about girls and parenting daughters of any age

Darling Daughters
www.darlingdaughters.org
Join us! Latest *Darling Daughters* Directory updates, a blog and forum for all of us to share stories and advice about raising our darling daughters.

My Daughter
www.mydaughter.co.uk
Advice from head teachers and other experts to help you with issues like education and friendships.

A Mighty Girl
www.amightygirl.com
Parenting tips and recommendations on books and films.

Everyday Sexism Project
www.everydaysexism.com
A live feed where anyone can post his or her story, no matter how seemingly insignificant, of a sexist experience. There is an accompanying book: *Everyday Sexism* by Laura Bates (Simon and Schuster, 2014).

Her Story
@herstory_uk
Engaging young people with women's history that is absent from the school curriculum. Follow on Twitter and a website is coming.

Antenatal advice
ParentSkool
www.parentskool.co.uk

Provides a wonderful approach and classes on birthing options, becoming a parent and beyond.

National Childbirth Trust
www.nct.org.uk
A national network of antenatal classes and website support for birth, breast feeding and parenting.

Baby darlings (0-2 years)
The Breastfeeding Network
www.breastfeedingnetwork.org.uk
An independent source of help and advice for anyone interested in breastfeeding and for those caring for breastfeeding mothers.

The Association for Postnatal Illness
www.apni.org
Advice, support and a helpline for anyone suffering postnatal illness, which affects approximately ten per cent of all recently delivered mothers.

Home Start
www.homestart.org.uk
Offers home visits, support and advice to parents with children under five.

Cry-sis
www.cry-sis.org.uk
Offers a daily helpline and support on sleepless and crying babies.

Children's sleep specialist
www.andreagrace.co.uk
Effective and gentle solutions bespoke to you and your baby.

Children and teens

The Kids Coach
www.thekidscoach.org.uk
Naomi offers coaching for children (6+) in person or by Skype, plus lots of resources for parents.

Teenagers – Sarah Newton
www.sarahnewton.com
Sarah specialises in offering coaching and support to teenagers, and their parents.

Exams, stress and performance coaching
www.cambridgeacademicperformance.co.uk
Liz Parker coaches teens and students with practical strategies to succeed and build their confidence.

Parenting advice and support

Parenting People
www.parentingpeople.co.uk
Parenting courses, workshops and individual parent coaching run by yours truly, Judy Reith.

The Parent Coaching Academy
www.theparentcoachingacademy.com
Founder Lorraine Thomas is one of the best coaches around.

The Parent Practice
www.theparentpractice.com
Offers parenting courses, talks and training for facilitators.

Sue Atkins

www.sueatkinsparentingcoach.com

Sue offers coaching, workshops and free resources for parents.

Parent Champions

www.parentchampioncommunity.com

The founder Alan Wilson offers a range of support services including online and face-to-face courses.

Parenting UK

www.parentinguk.org

Information on recognised parenting course providers in the UK. Parenting UK are creators of Parentchannel.tv (an online service) that has video clips on a good range of parenting issues.

Family Lives

www.familylives.org.uk

Leading charity offering a helpline and web chat service, plus online information for any parenting concerns.

NSPCC

NSPCC helpline (for adults) www.nspcc.org.uk/what-you-can-do/

This national body has a helpline for parents and another for children. It also offers resources, information and courses.

ChildLine

www.childline.org.uk

Twins and multiple births

www.tamba.org.uk

Help, advice and information on local networks for parents with twins or multiple births.

Children with additional or temporary needs

Attention Deficit Disorder, Attention Deficit Hyperactivity Disorder
www.adders.org
Resources, information, and support groups.

Children with disabilities

Contact a Family
www.cafamily.org.uk
Charity that supports children with disabilities and their families.

Bereavement

Winston's Wish
www.winstonswish.org.uk
Provides help and support to bereaved children.
Cruse
www.cruse.org.uk
A bereavement helpline, individual counselling or local group support for adults and children.

Secret 2: resource for single parents

Gingerbread
www.gingerbread.org.uk
Leading support, advice and campaigning charity for single parents.

Secret 3: V-signs resources

General
For books dealing in a general way with the V-signs, please refer to the Book and Movie Club (see page 265).
Personal, Social Health and Economic Association
www.pshe-association.org.uk
A platform that offers guidance, advice and lots of useful websites on drugs, alcohol, sex and relationships.

V is for Virtual – advice about technology

Technology Expert
www.carrick-davies.com/
Steve Carrick Davies is a dad, passionate speaker and trainer who has great ideas for helping parents understand the pros and cons of technology and how to regulate it.

YouTube
A clip, titled *Girls You Think You Know*, is a story about a girl, Internet safety and being groomed. The clip was produced by the Child Exploitation and Online Protection Centre (CEOP).
https://www.youtube.com/watch?v=vp5nScG6C5g

Child Net
www.childnet.com
Useful guides for parents, children and teachers.

Vodafone Digital Parenting
www.vodafone.com/content/parents/get-started.html
Comprehensive age-related guides about keeping children safe when they use technology.

ParentPort
www.parentport.org.uk
If you have seen, read or heard something on any form of media that you consider unsuitable for children, contact the ParentPort. Run by UK media regulators, it also offers advice for parents.

V is for Violins - advice about self-esteem

Mental health
www.youngminds.org.uk
Help and advice for parents and children.
MindFull
www.mindfull.org/
Mindfulness advice and information.

Dove Self-Esteem Project (Unilever)
www.dove.us/social-mission/self-esteem-toolkit-and-resources/
Information, which is geared for parents, teachers and mentors, about boosting young girls' self-esteem and understanding body image issues.

V is for Veruca Salt - advice on bitches and bullies

www.bullying.co.uk
Advice and helpline for parents.

Dr Michele Borba
www.micheleborba.com/Pages/ArtNLM03.htm
A good and comprehensive guide for parents on different kinds of friendship issues and how to help.

Bullying Prevention Headquarters
www.heyugly.org
Empowers and helps those suffering from bullying.

Kidscape
www.kidscape.org.uk
Information and tools for dealing with bullies and a helpline for parents.

ChildLine (NSPCC)
0800 1111
A call-in service for children to use. The motto is: No problem is too big or too small.

V is for Vomit and Vaginas – advice on nutrition, alcohol and other drugs, self-harm, puberty, sex and sexuality.

Eating disorders and nutrition
Beat
www.b-eat.co.uk
Helpline and national network of support groups for any eating disorder.

Nutritionist Resource Network
www.nutritionist-resource.org.uk
A comprehensive site of nutrition information and a directory of nutritionists.

Alcohol and other drugs
Frank
www.talktofrank.com
Help and advice for parents and teens on all drugs.

Breakthru Alcohol and Drug Awareness
www.breakthru.co.uk
A cross-community helpline and information organisation.

Drinkaware
www.drinkaware.co.uk/about-us
Information with age-related tips and support on alcohol misuse
and harm.

Self-harm
Harmless
www.harmless.org.uk
Advice and information on self-harm for parents and children.

Puberty, sex and relationships
NHS
www.nhs.uk/Livewell/Sexandyoungpeople/Pages/Girlspuberty.aspx
Good, clear information that will help parents and daughters get to
grips with puberty.

NHS
www.nhs.uk/conditions/Sexually-transmitted-infections/Pages/
Introduction.aspx
Good information on safer sex and sexually transmitted diseases
(STIs) for parents and daughters.

Family Planning
www.fpa.org.uk/Homepage
Keep up with the latest information on family planning.

Lesbian, gay and bisexual help
Stonewall
www.stonewall.org.uk/at_school/education_for_all/parents_and_
carers/4162.asp
Lesbian, gay and bisexual information, resources and help page for
parents.

Secret 4: resources for dads

Dad Talk
www.dad.info/about-us
Advice and support from pregnancy onwards, including a helpful concise timeline of what happens as pregnancy progresses.

Commando Dad
www.commandodad.com
Resources and a forum for new dads.

Fatherhood Institute
www.fatherhoodinstitute.org
Campaigns, research and resources for dads.

Families Need Fathers
www.fnf.org.uk
Offers help and a network of meetings for separated dads wanting to maintain contact with their children.

Secret 5: resources for mums

Mumsnet
www.mumsnet.com
Popular parenting website with discussion boards on every topic imaginable by parents for parents. Mumsnet Academy offers short courses and workshops on a range of topics.

Netmums
www.netmums.com
Parenting advice, information and courses.

Meet a Mum
www.mama.org.uk
Advice and networking for mums who feel isolated or who are suffering from postnatal depression.

Mum and Working
www.mumandworking.co.uk
A job site with advice on services that support working parents.

Working Mums
www.workingmums.co.uk
A recruitment site for mums with expert advice offered through the Q&A panel.

Health and relationships for parents and families
Janey Lee Grace
www.imperfectlynatural.com
Amazing source of easy to use alternative health and nutrition - books and website and PR training.

Couples counselling - Relate
www.relate.org.uk
National network of counsellors trained to support couples, and for children living in families with relationship problems.

Domestic violence: Women's Aid
www.womensaid.org.uk
Helpline and advice for those at risk from domestic violence.

Secret 6: resources for building a supportive village

Schools
Girls' School Association
www.gsa.uk.com

My Daughter
www.mydaughter.co.uk

Volunteering England
www.volunteering.org.uk

Volunteering Wales
www.volunteering-wales.net

Volunteering Scotland
www.volunteerscotland.net

Northern Ireland
www.volunteernow.co.uk
Networks of resources and volunteering information.

Book and Movie Club

A selection of the favourites in our family are listed below. Age recommendations are a guide only. If you're not sure, read or watch the title first yourself – you know your daughter best and what she will enjoy or what could be too much for her.

If you want more suggestions, there is a great website full of recommendations for darlings of all ages www.amightygirl.com

Little darlings (3–7 years)

All featuring strong, resourceful and independent minded female characters.

Movies
Frozen (Walt Disney Animation Studio, 2013)
Brave (Pixar Animation Studios, 2012)
Mulan (Walt Disney Feature Animation, 1998)
Mary Poppins (Walt Disney, 1964)
The Sound of Music (Robert Wise, 1965)

Books
Peace at Last, Jill Murphy (Walker Books, 1980; Macmillan Children's Books, 1999)
The Owl Babies, Martin Waddell and Patrick Benson (Walker Books, 1975)
Milly-Molly-Mandy, Joyce Lankester Brisley (Puffin, re-issued 1973)
A series of books about a fun, inquisitive and generous girl from a happy family.
My Naughty Little Sister, Dorothy Edwards and Shirley Hughes (First published 1952. Egmont, re-issue 2010)
A much-loved series of books. Follow the reading of a story with an empathic chat about annoying siblings!
The Deep, Tim Winton (Penguin Books, 1999)
A great tale about overcoming fears, in this case swimming in the sea.
Who Made Me?, Malcolm Doney and Meryl Doney (Candle Books 2006)
A wonderful introduction to the facts of life!
Hair in Funny Places, Babette Cole (Red Fox, 2001)
A beautiful tale of a girl and her teddy and what happens when Mr and Mrs Hormone wake up and cause havoc in the girl's body.

Amazing Grace, Mary Hoffman (Francis Lincoln, 2007)
A tale about how a grandmother's wisdom shows a girl how to be whoever she wants to be.

Older darlings (8–12 years)

Matilda, Roald Dahl (Puffin, re-issue 2013)
Book-loving Matilda is willing to be different and challenge her awful family!
Anne of Green Gables, L. M. Montgomery (Wordsworth Classics, first published 1908)
A good one for anyone teased for having red hair. Anne is a strong and lively girl who survives many mishaps and thrives in the academic world.
His Dark Materials, Philip Pullman (Scholastic, 1995–2000)
Lyra is headstrong, feisty and a questioner in this epic trilogy!
The Hunger Games, Suzanne Collins
Book trilogy and film series where the character Katniss Everdeen displays loyalty, toughness and intelligence.
The Diary of a Young Girl, Anne Frank
The diary of a resilient, brave and resourceful girl hiding from the Nazis.
Whale Rider, Witi Ihimaera
The story is about a 12-year-old Maori girl who is a nature lover and follows her instincts and knows her own mind.
Harry Potter series, J. K. Rowling (Bloomsbury Publishing, 1997–2007)
Hermione Granger, the main female character, is clever and a good friend.
Jacqueline Wilson
A prolific writer of children's stories that tackle tough issues, such as adoption, divorce and mental health.

Young ladies (from 13 years)

The 7 Habits of Highly Effective Teens, Sean Covey (Touchstone Books, 1998)
A very useful self-help guide for teens on developing life skills.
Oranges Are Not the Only Fruit (1985) and *Why Be Happy When You Could be Normal?* (2012), Jeanette Winterson
An excellent writer whose love of books and writing helped her overcome a sad and destructive childhood.
The Fault in Our Stars, John Green (Penguin, 2013)
The story provides a good model for building relationships and dealing with adversity.
Divergent, Veronica Roth (HarperCollins Children's Books, 2011)
A popular book and more recently a film where the heroine Tris Prior faces tough decisions on life, death and love.
To Kill a Mockingbird, Harper Lee (First published 1960)
A much-loved coming of age novel that is centred on a 1930s rape case involving a white woman and a black man. The unfolding story is seen through the eyes of the defending lawyer's young children.
Jane Eyre, Charlotte Brontë (First published 1847)
A moving classic in which Jane confronts her miserable childhood, stands up for strong feminist principles and deals with the complications of being in love with her employer.
Wuthering Heights, Emily Brontë (First published 1847)
A complicated tale of love and revenge centred on the characters of free-spirited Catherine Earnshaw and tortured romantic hero Heathcliff.
Pride and Prejudice, Jane Austen (First published 1813)
Elizabeth Bennet deals with love, morality and the role of a woman in nineteenth-century England.
Noughts and Crosses series, Malorie Blackman (Corgi, 2006)
Award-winning dramatic tales involving racial issues, adventure and romance.

Books for parents of daughters

Raising Girls, Steve Biddulph (Harper Thorsons, 2013)

21st Century Girls, Sue Palmer (Orion Books, 2013)

What Should We Tell Our Daughters?, Melissa Benn (Hodder & Stoughton, 2013)

Decoding Your 21st Century Daughter, Helen Wright, (emBooks, 2013)

Raising Confident Girls, Ian Grant and Mary Grant, (Vermilion, 2009)

Raising Girls, Gisela Preuschoff (Harper Thorsons, 2005)

How Jane Won, Dr Sylvia Rimm (Crown New York, 2001)

The Wonder of Girls, Michael Gurian (Atria Books, Simon & Schuster, 2003)

You Don't Really Know Me, Dr Terri Apter (W. W. Norton & Co, 2005)

How To Be A Woman, Caitlin Moran (Ebury Press, 2012)

Your Daughter, the Girls' School Association, (The Friday Project, 2011)

Secondary School – A Parent's Guide, Glynis Kozma (Need2Know, 2013)

The Female Brain, Louann Brizendine MD (Bantam Books, 2008)

Confident Teens, Gael Lindenfield (Thorsons, 2011)

The Curse of the Good Girl, Rachel Simmons (Penguin Books, 2009)

The Parent's Toolkit , Naomi Richards (Vermilion, 2012)

I have included the following book as many readers will have sons and this is an excellent read.

Ten Conversations You Must Have With Your Son, Dr Tim Hawkes (Hachette, 2014)

Books for dads

Commando Dad, Neil Sinclair (Summersdale, 2010)
Fantastic First Time Father, Tim Mungeam (Quercus, 2013)
Top 50 tips for first time dads.
Fatherhood: The Truth, Marcus Berkmann (Vermilion, 2005)
This is a laugh out loud guide to becoming a dad.
Be A Great Dad, Andrew Watson (Hodder Education, 2010)
Teach yourself to be the world's best dad.

Books for mums

Be A Great Mum, Judy Reith (Hodder Education, 2008)
Time Management for Manic Mums; Get Control of Your Life In 7 Weeks, Allison Mitchell (Hay House, 2012)
The Mum's Guide to Returning to Work, Bekki Clark (Lulu.com, 2011)

Books for separating parents

The Guide for Separated Parents, Karen Woodall, Nick Woodall, (Piatkus 2009)
Family Breakdown, Penelope Leach (Unbound, 2014)

Birth order

Remember that your children are unique. This information provides guidelines only.

- Birth order is significant as it can feature throughout our lives influencing our work, our relationships and how we treat our children.
- An age gap of three years or less between siblings makes birth order more significant. A gap of greater than three years

increases the likelihood of a child having only child or firstborn characteristics.

- Don't make the assumption that your children will be similar to you and your siblings. For example, avoid comparisons such as: 'They fight just like my sister and I did.'
- Lots of fights? Set up separate activities with each child. One-to-one time, even just a few minutes, can really help.
- When you're with one child, don't compare him or her to a sibling or talk about his or her siblings.
- Let a child spend time with other families – related or not – where his or her position is different. For example, a firstborn child could spend time being the youngest among older cousins.
- Parents are likely to change with the birth of each child. You are both older, possibly more affluent and likely to be more relaxed. Your values could have changed since your firstborn. What was important first time round is no longer a priority.

Only child characteristics

High achiever, keen to please and thinks that he or she is special, powerful and capable (especially a girl). Is likely to be assertive. An only child may prefer to have several children when he or she has their own family.

HOWEVER, an only child can feel it is a burden to be a 'credit' to parents who may be overprotective, especially physically. This child may mature too soon and find conflict hard to resolve. The family atmosphere may be claustrophobic, so he or she seeks space.

Firstborn characteristics

This child has his or her parents' undivided attention (similar to an only child) for a period, especially if the age gap is three years plus to the nearest sibling. He or she could be academic, a natural leader, assertive, task orientated, analytical and responsible. He or she could relate well to authority figures.

HOWEVER, a firstborn may resent responsibility and could more likely become a 'problem' child who is vulnerable to stress. This child may feel that he or she has to take charge if parents are weak. He or she may tell tales, and often seeks approval.

Later and middle-born characteristics

Parents tend to be more relaxed and take more risks. This child may have strong social skills, be flexible (good for forming relationships later in life). He or she may be trusting, accepting, aesthetic, artistic, a team player, 'other' centred, humorous and enjoy outdoor pursuits.

HOWEVER, he or she may feel 'squeezed in the middle' once a younger sibling is born and be not sure who he or she is. The child may recognise he or she no longer has oldest or youngest privileges. This child may not take into account the age gap being the reason he or she isn't as capable as an older sibling. A middle-born child can be a 'problem child' who seeks to gain attention.

Last-born characteristics

This child can feel a strong sense of security and can play up to the role of being 'the baby'. He or she can have the highest level of self-esteem, lack a competitive streak and may expect others to take responsibility. Able to follow a routine that is established by someone else, but may not be able to make one for him- or herself. This child needs clear instructions and expectations.

HOWEVER, the last-born can be spoiled by parents and siblings and indulged with flexible bedtimes or extra pocket money, for example. He or she may not be taken seriously or given exclusive love and attention. The latter can result in needing a lot more attention in key relationships in his or her later life.

> *I prefer it when my parents spend time with me without my sister, even if it's just having a movie night while she stays at a friend's house because it makes me feel that they are still thinking about me.*

Jodie, aged 15

How to learn to listen

66 Always listen to what your daughter has to say; notice if she isn't as lively as she usually is. 99

Hettie, aged 10

Before you say anything think about who you can talk to when you are upset or have a dilemma. Whoever it is, he or she is likely to be a great listener who makes you feel accepted understood, cared for and trusted. How do they do that? Here are some guidelines.

Offer time to listen. Turn off distractions. Be fed, watered and not too tired! Sit down if you can opposite your daughter. Go for eye contact unless you can see it is not wanted.

You can listen when doing something together - driving in the car, walking, clearing up the kitchen or when she is in bed relaxing before going to sleep. Breathe steadily and keep your body relaxed, arms unfolded.

Your attitude

How are you? If you're too upset or you find yourself making unhelpful judgements and wanting to interrupt, wait until you have calmed down before attempting to listen. Notice what stops you listening too.

If your daughter is crying or very upset, wait a little while rubbing her back.

Offering tissues can be perceived as the tears making you feel uncomfortable, but go with your instincts.

Choose your words

Feelings are more important than content.

- **Something wrong?** Try a gentle question with a guess at how she might be feeling. For example: 'You seem upset about something. I've noticed you've been spending a lot of time in your room.'
- **Try an invitation to talk.** Use 'door openers' like who, what, when or how? For example, 'How was the journey home? When would be a good time to talk about what's worrying you?'
- **Silence might be golden.** Notice how much you're tempted to jump in and fill silence with suggestions and questions. A lot is happening in the silence, be patient.
- **Use open-ended questions** such as 'How does that make you feel?'
- **Sum up what your daughter has said.** Paraphrasing will help her feel heard, and may clarify anything you have misunderstood. For example: 'So you forgot your phone and missed the text about the party?'
- **Reflect contents and feelings** by saying something like 'I guess that was hard being left out?'

Avoid:
- Closed questions that can only be answered yes or no, such as 'Are you upset?'
- Questions that demand information, such as 'Tell me what he said?'
- Reassuring platitudes like 'You'll be fine, it'll soon blow over.'
- Imposing solutions, such as 'You must talk to him and sort this out.'
- Advice or 'me toos' – offering advice takes the power away from your daughter to come up with her own solutions. 'Me toos', such as 'I know just how you feel. That happened to me too' takes the conversation away from your daughter and focuses it on you.

Moving on
- Invite your daughter to say what she thinks she could do or say.
- Brainstorm ideas together, but let her do most of the talking.
- If your daughter is really struggling, you could suggest what you might do if you were in her shoes.

66 My parents were great at listening, understanding and forgiving. 99

Elaine, now in her thirties

Chores your daughter can do and when

What follows is a list of typical tasks that parents do for their daughters (and their sons) but which she will need to be able to do for herself well before she leaves home. Learning how to do chores – and to carry on doing them – builds your daughter's self-esteem as you thank her and encourage her. It helps her learn and develop team skills, resilience, the value of effort, and the reward of doing a job properly.

Look at the list and think about how often *your daughter* does each of these chores independently and then tick Always, Sometimes or Never.

The ages are only an estimate, you know your daughter best. Some parents look at this with their daughter, or complete it separately and compare answers.

Little darlings (2–5 years)

	ALWAYS	SOMETIMES	NEVER
Gets up and dressed			
Makes bed and tidies room			
Baths, cleans teeth and brushes hair			
Manages personal hygiene			
Helps in the kitchen			
Supervises own food or drinks			
Clears away plates and cups			
Tidies, vacuums or dusts			
Changes loo roll			

Young darlings (6–10 years)
All of the above, plus:

	ALWAYS	SOMETIMES	NEVER
Helps with laundry			
Folds and puts away clean clothes			
Helps with the shopping			
Helps with gardening or pet care			
Helps to choose or buy her own clothes			

Older darlings (from 11 years)
All of the above, plus:

	ALWAYS	SOMETIMES	NEVER
Organises homework			
Manages her own time			
Plans everything needed for her own outings			
Manages her money			

Is there one area of responsibility that you could introduce to your daughter this week? Her effort, however small, is what you're looking for; not perfection or an opportunity to give her a lecture. Thank her for her efforts and be specific: 'You did the dishes, thanks,' rather than, 'You're so helpful.' Consider the ticks on the list and make a plan, asking yourself these questions:

What chore can my daughter start doing?
When will you discuss this with her?
How will you demonstrate the chore?

Please review this list as your daughter grows up. It's amazing how many parents I meet who are still changing the loo roll for their grown-up darlings.

Parents' Notes
Write it down. Make it happen!

Dear Reader,

I hope *7 Secrets of Raising Girls Every Parent Must Know* is helping you and your daughter. However, making notes as you go through each secret will make this book become your story. Record what information or observance has struck a chord and what changes you wish to make. Fill these blank pages with jotted notes, doodles, pictures and mind maps to help your learning and reflections come alive for you, now and in the future.

Secret 1: Change

Understand and prepare for how your darling daughter grows up

What made you pick up *7 Secrets of Raising Girls Every Parent Must Know* and what do you hope to learn from reading it?

What do you enjoy about having a daughter the stage she is currently at?

....

....

....

What are the biggest challenges?

....

....

....

What's the one thing you would pass on to a parent with a child in the previous age group to the one you're in now?

....

....

....

Secret 2: Values

Live by your legacy to your daughter

Think about ten qualities you want to demonstrate as a parent – fairness, honesty, patience and hard work, for example.

As a parent, I want to be…

1. ....

2. ....

3. ....

4. ....

5. ....

6. ....

7. ....

8. ....

9. ....

10. ....

It's important that your values are not just words, but are alive and working. You might want to score your values out of ten, with ten being: 'I am completely satisfied with how this value is present in my parenting.' A zero score could mean that a value is absent in your parenting.

Write your parenting story about what you want to leave behind for your daughter. You could think about the life lessons that the actor Bob Hoskins left for his daughter.

....

....

....

What are you taking away from the second secret?

....

....

....

Secret 3: V-SIGNS

Know what is essential to keep your darling daughter safe and happy

Start by acknowledging what your worries are about your daughter. It may be helpful to look at the list on page 96. Remember mental, emotional, physical and spiritual concerns can overlap. A physical concern, such as a weight issue, is likely to be a mental and an emotional issue too.

Mental? (For example, 'She thinks we prefer her older sister.')

....

....

....

Emotional? (For example, 'She is anxious about our house move.')

....

....

....

Physical? (For example, 'She eats too much sugar.')

....

....

....

Spiritual? (For example, 'She has taken up a religion we're worried about.')

....

....

....

In your family what screen time is allowed and when?

....

....

....

What rules around technology are you going to set? Involve your daughter in this family discussion. Include coming up with ideas about what to do when it's time to put technology away.

....

....

....

Who or what is putting pressure on your daughter?

....

....

....

What can you do to boost your daughter's self-esteem?

....

....

....

What's happening for my daughter in relation to friendships? What action (if any) do I need to take?

....

....

....

What concerns do I have about my daughter's body or her attitude towards it? What action (if any) do I need to take?

....

....

....

What are you taking away from the third secret?

....

....

....

SECRET 4: Dads

Use your power wisely.

What will help remind you to live out your values? Is it a picture, a drawing, a photo, some words, a memento or a piece of music?

....

....

....

What or who causes you to feel guilty?

....

....

....

Imagine guilt has gone. What thoughts, ideas and actions would you replace it with?

....

....

....

What did you love to do before kids came along?

....

....

....

What was it about that interest that you enjoyed?

....

....

....

What could you do to bring it back into your life now, even in a reduced version?

....

....

....

What are you taking away from the fourth secret?

....

....

....

SECRET 5: Mums

Ditch the guilt! Be the role model you want your daughter to have.
What activity (or inactivity!) that is within your control would give you a boost? Identify five things in each of these time slots.

If I had five minutes for myself I would:

....

....

....

....

If I had a few hours for myself I would:

....

....

....

....

If I had a day or more for myself I would:

....

....

....

....

Write a letter to your daughter spelling out everything that you want her to learn from you.

To my darling daughter,

....

....

....

....

All my love,

Mum xxxx

What are the hopes, fears and expectations about your daughter's career?

....

....

....

What am I prepared to offer to support her to find a career?

....

....

....

What do I do if she chooses a career path that raises concerns for us?

....

....

....

Guilt is a terrible drain on energy and it wrecks confidence. What or who is causing your guilt?

....

....

....

Who are the Marmars in your life?

....

....

....

If you can, make some notes about what your mum or other women, perhaps from a previous generation, have given you, and your daughter.

....

....

....

What are you taking away from the fifth secret?

....

....

....

Secret 6: Build your village

Create a community to help you and your daughter.

Make a list, draw a mind map or a doodle to answer these questions.

Who is helping my daughter to grow up well, apart from her parents?

....

....

Who loves her?

....

....

....

Who shows an interest in her?

....

....

....

Who listens to her?

....

....

....

Who teaches her life skills?

....

....

....

Who can she trust?

....

....

....

Who is kind to her?

....

....

....

Who encourages her?

....

....

....

Ask your daughter which adults she admires and why. Note her answers here and use them to help you consider who is missing from her village.

....

....

....

How can you build a village for yourself? They are delicate questions. Take care as you consider them.

Who loves you?

....

....

....

Who shows an interest in you?

....

....

....

Who listens to you?

....

....

....

Who do you trust?

....

....

....

Who is kind to you?

....

....

....

Who encourages you?

....

....

....

Who helps you with practical day-to-day things?

....

....

....

What is your education wish list for your daughter?

....

....

....

What do you believe educating girls is for? (If you have sons too, this will illuminate if you have different beliefs about how you would answer this question.)

....

....

....

What are your best memories of school?

....

....

....

What do you want from the schools where your daughter will spend 13 or so years of her life?

....

....

....

What are the most important values that you want to find in action in the schools your daughter attends?

....

....

....

What are your views on paying for education? Never? Maybe? Definitely?

....

....

....

What is your educational legacy (excluding schooling) to your daughter?

....

....

....

What are you taking away from the sixth secret?

....

....

....

Secret 7: PATIENCE

You are a parent forever – there is no rush.

What would your parenting be like if you had more patience?

....

....

....

What are your View-Master moments? To refresh your memory on this, turn to pages 240–244.

....

....

....

What are you taking away from the seventh secret?

....

....

....

Review

Look back at the notes you made when you started reading *7 Secrets of Raising Girls Every Parent Must Know*. What changes have you made as a parent of a daughter as a result of reading this book?

....

....

....

Which is your favourite secret and why?

....

....

....

Thanks for taking up your precious time to make notes, I'm sure you'll find your reflections a fascinating read in the future when you and your daughter have moved on to a new phase. Meanwhile, share the secrets and keep in touch with the Darling Daughters village at www.darlingdaughters.org.

INDEX

ACKNOWLEDGEMENTS

My village:

Adrian – best boy

Liz and Nancy – best sisters

My book village

I am hugely grateful to these kind souls who have given their time, talent and listening ears to help me bring *7 Secrets of Raising Girls Every Parent Must Know* to life.

Jane Graham Maw and Jennifer Christie at GMC – best agent.

Anna Martin and Claire Plimmer – best publishers.

Lyn Murray – best attention to detail.

Hannah Cousins – best illustrator.

Ruby Wroe - best photographer.

Plus: Jeanette Aboujieb, Hugh Dennis, Ali Hewson, Janey Lee Grace, Carol Smillie, Simon Mayo, Hilary Mayo, Martin Wroe, Meg Wroe, Jacqui Christian, Karen Napier, Brita and Ed Wolf, Malcolm and Meryl Doney, Angela Reith, Jo Browning Wroe, Helen Robbins, Dr Tim Hawkes, Steph Hoskin, Justine Roberts and the Mumsnet Academy team, Sarah Rose, Willie Williams, Bev Sage, Zoe Sinclair, Nick Welsh.

Darling schools: St John's College School, St Mary's School, Stephen Perse Foundation (Cambridge).

All the mums, dads and daughters who gave their ideas to make *7 Secrets of Raising Girls Every Parent Must Know* a much better read.

Please keep the *Darling Daughters* village growing at www.darlingdaughters.org.

A percentage of profits from sales of this book will be donated to The Street Child World Cup, a global event for street children under the care of leading street child charities in each country taking part. It uses this event (and many other events) to highlight the rights of all children to education and safety.

'No child should have to live on the streets.'

www.streetchildworldcup.org

NOTES

....
....
....
....
....
....
....
....
....
....
....
....
....
....
....
....
....
....
....
....
....
....
....

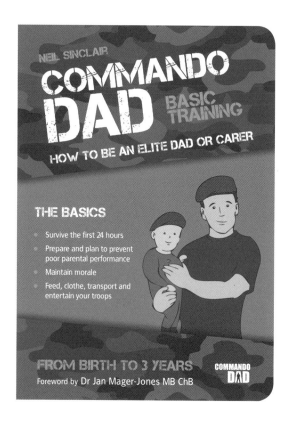

'one of the best parenting books I've ever read'
Lorraine Kelly

'The advice, approved by healthcare professionals, is
quick to read, easy to understand and simple to digest,
delivered in short, unambiguous bullet points and, no-
nonsense rules – and, pretty unarguably, spot on.'
THE GUARDIAN

'A must-have for new dads'
MADE magazine

COMMANDO DAD
How to be an elite dad or carer

ISBN: 978 1 84953 261 7   Paperback   £10.99

ATTENTION

In your hand is an indispensable training manual for new recruits to fatherhood. Written by ex-Commando and dad of three, Neil Sinclair, this manual will teach you, in no-nonsense terms, how to:

- Plan for your baby trooper's arrival
- Prepare nutritious food for your unit
- Deal with hostilities in the ranks
- Maintain morale and keep the troops entertained

And much, much more.

Let Training Commence!

Also available:

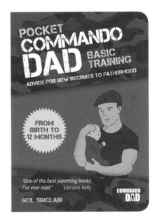

POCKET COMMANDO DAD
Advice for new recruits to fatherhood

ISBN: 978 1 84953 555 7
Paperback
£7.99

NEW *Old-Fashioned* PARENTING

A GUIDE TO HELP YOU FIND THE BALANCE
BETWEEN TRADITIONAL AND MODERN PARENTING

LIAT HUGHES JOSHI

NEW OLD-FASHIONED PARENTING
A guide to help you find the balance
between traditional and modern parenting

ISBN: 978 1 84953 672 1   Paperback   £10.99

There's been a revolution in the
family; it's now all about the kids.

We've moved on from children being 'seen and not heard', but we're now
plagued with the worry of ending up with 'that child' – the one who's running
amok and is ill-prepared for life.

This book combines contemporary and traditional childrearing methods,
bringing fresh thinking to some of the essential parenting issues of our time:

- Managing screen use
- Encouraging independence
- Finding the balance between school and play
- Compromising between parenting that's pushy and not involved enough
- Establishing the 'best of both worlds' approach that works in the modern
  world for modern families.

In this manifesto of new old-fashioned parenting there's no pandering, no
spoiling, and definitely no dinosaur-shaped chicken nuggets at dinner time.

*'The antidote to over-indulgent modern parenting. Challenges some of the
ways we've come to think about what's best for our children and provides
fresh, practical advice about parenting dilemmas of our times.'*

Oliver James, psychologist and author of
Affluenza and *How Not to F*** Them Up*

If you're interested in finding out more about our books,
find us on Facebook at **Summersdale Publishers** and follow us
on Twitter at **@Summersdale**.

www.summersdale.com